An Introduction to State
Space Time Series Analysis

D1599255

Practical Econometrics

Series Editors
Jurgen Doornik and Bronwyn Hall

Practical econometrics is a series of books designed to provide accessible and practical introductions to various topics in econometrics. From econometric techniques to econometric modelling approaches, these short introductions are ideal for applied economists, graduate students, and researchers looking for a non-technical discussion on specific topics in econometrics.

An Introduction to State Space Time Series Analysis

Jacques J. F. Commandeur
Siem Jan Koopman

OXFORD
UNIVERSITY PRESS

OXFORD

UNIVERSITY PRESS

Great Clarendon Street, Oxford ox2 6DP

Oxford University Press is a department of the University of Oxford.
It furthers the University's objective of excellence in research, scholarship,
and education by publishing worldwide in

Oxford New York

Auckland Cape Town Dar es Salaam Hong Kong Karachi
Kuala Lumpur Madrid Melbourne Mexico City Nairobi
New Delhi Shanghai Taipei Toronto

With offices in

Argentina Austria Brazil Chile Czech Republic France Greece
Guatemala Hungary Italy Japan Poland Portugal Singapore
South Korea Switzerland Thailand Turkey Ukraine Vietnam

Oxford is a registered trademark of Oxford University Press
in the UK and in certain other countries

Published in the United States
by Oxford University Press Inc., New York

British Library Cataloguing in Publication Data
Data available

Library of Congress Cataloging in Publication Data
Data available

Typeset by SPI Publisher Services, Pondicherry, India
Printed in Great Britain
on acid-free paper by
Biddles Ltd., King's Lynn, Norfolk

ISBN 978–0–19–922887–4

1 3 5 7 9 10 8 6 4 2

Preface

This book provides an introductory treatment of state space methods applied to unobserved-component time series models which are also known as structural time series models. The book started as a collection of personal notes made by JJFC about what he discovered and understood while studying state space methods for the first time. When colleagues and friends also found these notes useful and helpful, the idea came up to make them publicly available. SJK started to cooperate with JJFC on this book project as part of the highly enjoyable joint projects for the SWOV Institute for Road Safety Research in Leidschendam, the Netherlands.

Harvey (1989) and Durbin and Koopman (2001) treat the topic of state space methods at an advanced level suitable for postgraduate and advanced graduate courses in time series analysis. Elementary time series books, on the other hand, provide only very limited space to the class of unobserved-component models. Most of the attention is given to the Box–Jenkins approach to time series analysis.

The intended audience for this book is practitioners and researchers working in areas other than statistics, but who use time series on a daily basis in areas such as the social sciences, quantitative history, biology and medicine. This book offers a step-by-step approach to the analysis of the salient features in time series such as the trend, seasonal and irregular components. Practical problems such as forecasting and missing values are treated in some detail. The book may also serve as an accompanying textbook for a basic time series course in econometrics and statistics, typically at an undergraduate level.

JJFC would like to acknowledge and thank the management and the colleagues of the SWOV Institute for Road Safety Research for their mental and financial contribution to this publication. The book is an important component of the SWOV Research Programme 2003–2006.

Among all SWOV colleagues, JJFC is especially indebted to Frits Bijleveld, whose never abating and infectious enthusiasm for state space methods was instrumental in stimulating JJFC to write this book. He was always willing to answer any questions JJFC had, and is a genius in exploiting the enormous flexibility that state space methods have to offer.

The authors are grateful to a referee for his positive remarks on an earlier draft of the book. His many constructive comments have improved the book considerably. Any mistakes and omissions remain the sole responsibility of the authors.

JJFC also wishes to thank members (some of them, former members) of the International Co-operation on Time Series Analysis (ICTSA): Peter Christens, Ruth Bergel, Joanna Zukowska, Filip Van den Bossche, Geert Wets, Stefan Hoeglinger, Ward Vanlaar, Phillip Gould, Max Cameron, and Stewart Newstead, for their inspiring contributions to our in-depth discussions on time series analysis, and for their encouraging response to earlier drafts of the book.

SJK would like to thank his colleagues at the Department of Econometrics, Vrije Universiteit Amsterdam, for giving him the opportunity to work on this book.

The book was written in LaTeX using the MiKTeX system (http://www.miktex.org). We thank Frits Bijleveld for his assistance in setting up the LaTeX system. The Ox and SsfPack code for carrying out the analyses discussed in the book, as well as the data files, can be downloaded from http://staff.feweb.vu.nl/koopman and from http://www.ssfpack.com.

Contents

Contents

List of Figures

List of Tables

1

Introduction

This book introduces time series analysis using state space methodology to readers who are neither familiar with time series analysis nor with state space methods. The only background required in order to understand the material in this book is a basic knowledge of classical linear regression models, of which a condensed review is provided first. A few sections also assume familiarity with matrix algebra. These starred sections may however be skipped without losing the flow of the exposition.

In classical regression analysis a linear relationship is assumed between a criterion or dependent or endogenous variable y, and a predictor or independent or exogenous variable x. Deviations from this relationship are assumed to come from a random process (see Chapter 10 for the definition of a random process) centred at zero. The standard regression model for n observations of y (denoted by y_i for $i = 1, \ldots, n$) and x (denoted by x_i for $i = 1, \ldots, n$) is formally written as

$$y_i = a + b x_i + \varepsilon_i, \qquad \varepsilon_i \sim \text{NID}(0, \sigma_\varepsilon^2) \qquad (1.1)$$

for $i = 1, \ldots, n$. The statement

$$\varepsilon_i \sim \text{NID}(0, \sigma_\varepsilon^2) \qquad (1.2)$$

in (1.1) is shorthand notation for the assumption that the disturbances or errors or residuals ε_i are normally and independently distributed with mean equal to zero and variance equal to σ_ε^2.

The regression model (1.1) has three unknown coefficients that can be estimated by least squares methods. In particular, the least squares estimates of a and b, denoted by $\hat{a}$ and $\hat{b}$, respectively, are calculated by

$$\hat{b} = \sum_{i=1}^{n} (x_i - \bar{x}) y_i \, / \, \sum_{i=1}^{n} (x_i - \bar{x})^2, \qquad \hat{a} = \bar{y} - \hat{b}\bar{x},$$

where $\bar{y}$ and $\bar{x}$ are the sample means of y_i and x_i, respectively, for $i = 1, \ldots, n$. The least squares estimate of the disturbance variance σ_ε^2, denoted by $\hat{\sigma}_\varepsilon^2$, is calculated by

$$\hat{\sigma}_\varepsilon^2 = \sum_{i=1}^{n} (y_i - \hat{a} - \hat{b}x_i)^2 / (n-2).$$

More detailed discussions on least squares methods can be found in many textbooks on statistics and econometrics.

Suppose that the dependent variable y_i in (1.1) refers to the log of the monthly number of drivers killed or seriously injured (KSI) in the United Kingdom (UK) for the period January 1969 to December 1984. Since the period spans 16 years, we have $n = 16 \times 12 = 192$ observations and y_i is observed for $i = 1, \ldots, 192$. This set of observations for y_i can be referred to as a *time series* because it consists of repeated measurements in time of the same phenomenon. Further, suppose that the independent variable x_i in (1.1) is the index of time points in the series, that is $x_i = i = 1, 2, \ldots, 192$.

A scatter plot of variable y on x together with the best fitting line according to classical linear regression are presented in Figure 1.1. The

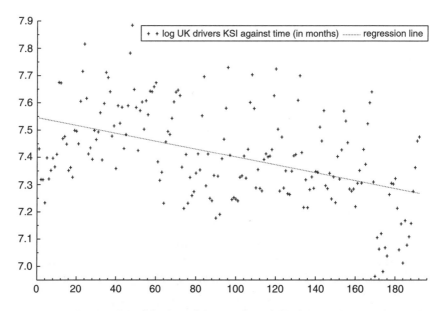

Figure 1.1. Scatter plot of the log of the number of UK drivers KSI against time (in months), including regression line.

equation of the regression line in Figure 1.1 is

$$\hat{y}_i = \hat{a} + \hat{b}x_i = 7.5458 - 0.00145\, x_i,$$

with error variance $\hat{\sigma}_\varepsilon^2 = 0.022998$. The standard F-test for fit yields $F_{(1,190)} = 53.775$ ($p < 0.001$), implying that the linear relationship between the criterion variable y and the predictor variable x is highly significant. Graphically, the intercept $\hat{a} = 7.5458$ in model (1.1) is the point where the regression line intersects with the y-axis, as is confirmed by inspection of Figure 1.1. Therefore, the intercept determines the *level* of the regression line on the y-axis. The value of the regression coefficient or weight $\hat{b} = -0.00145$ determines the *slope* of the regression line (i.e. the tangent of its angle with the x-axis).

Whether this analysis is satisfactory remains to be seen. We have established that time is a significant predictor of the log of the numbers of drivers KSI, and that there is a negative relation between these two variables: as time proceeds the log of the number of drivers killed or seriously injured decreases. However, a key assumption of classical regression analysis is not considered in the analysis. The observations y, after their correction for the intercept and the exogenous variable x, are assumed to be *independent* of each other. This is implied by (1.2). In the present example these observations are not independent because they are interrelated through *time*. This becomes more obvious by connecting the consecutive observations in Figure 1.1 with lines, as is illustrated in Figure 1.2. It shows that there is a systematic pattern in the time series y_i that can only partially be caught by the intercept and the time variable $x_i = i$. The residuals should be randomly distributed. However, Figure 1.3 shows that the residuals are clearly not randomly distributed.

A useful diagnostic tool for investigating the randomness of a set of observations is the *correlogram*. The correlogram is a graph containing correlations between an observed time series and the same time series shifted k time points into the future. Thus, the correlogram of the least squares errors $\hat{\epsilon}_i = y_i - \hat{a} - \hat{b}x_i$ in Figure 1.3 (which is also a time series) consists of the correlation between $\hat{\epsilon}_i$ and $\hat{\epsilon}_{i-1}$, the correlation between $\hat{\epsilon}_i$ and $\hat{\epsilon}_{i-2}$, the correlation between $\hat{\epsilon}_i$ and $\hat{\epsilon}_{i-3}$, and so on. Table 1.1 illustrates for some arbitrary numbers how the residuals are shifted in time in order to compute these correlations.

Using a more general notation, the correlogram contains the correlations between $\hat{\epsilon}_i$ and $\hat{\epsilon}_{i-k}$, for $k = 1, 2, 3, \ldots$. Since k equals the distance in time between the observations, it is called a *lag*. Moreover, since the

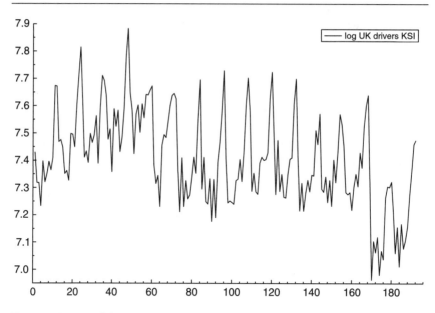

Figure 1.2. Log of the number of UK drivers KSI plotted as a time series.

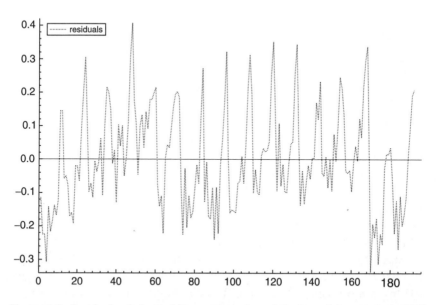

Figure 1.3. Residuals of classical linear regression of the log of the number of UK drivers KSI on time.

Table 1.1. Shifting of residuals for computation of autocorrelations.

i	$k = 0$ $\hat{\epsilon}_i$	1 $\hat{\epsilon}_{i-k}$	2 $\hat{\epsilon}_{i-k}$	3 $\hat{\epsilon}_{i-k}$
1	0.2	—	—	—
2	−0.4	0.2	—	—
3	0.0	−0.4	0.2	—
4	0.3	0.0	−0.4	0.2
5	−0.2	0.3	0.0	−0.4
6	0.1	−0.2	0.3	0.0

correlations are computed between a variable and itself (albeit shifted in time), they are called *autocorrelations*.

The correlogram of an independently distributed series of residuals is expected to consist of zeroes. In this case, the correlogram typically takes on the form shown in Figure 1.4. The two horizontal lines in the correlogram are the 95% confidence limits $\pm 2/\sqrt{n} = \pm 2/\sqrt{192} = \pm 0.144$. If residuals are randomly distributed then they are independent of one another. In the correlogram, the independence between random normally distributed residuals is reflected in the fact that all autocorrelations (of

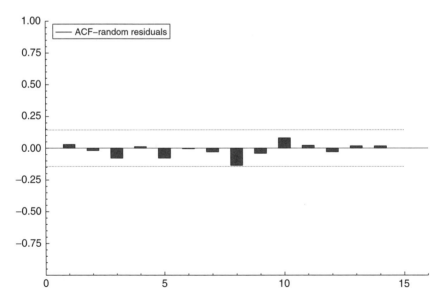

Figure 1.4. Correlogram of random time series.

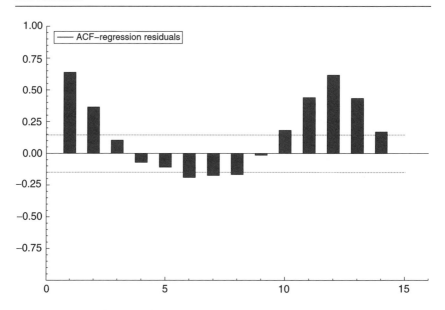

Figure 1.5. Correlogram of classical regression residuals.

which the first 14 are graphed in Figure 1.4) are close to zero, and do not exceed the confidence limits.

In contrast, the correlogram containing the first 14 autocorrelations of the classical regression residuals in Figure 1.3 takes on the form presented in Figure 1.5. The non-random nature of these residuals is confirmed by the fact that the correlogram in Figure 1.5 contains many autocorrelations significantly different from zero.

In principle, there is nothing wrong in fitting a classical regression model on the data in Figure 1.1 to obtain a rough idea of the linear trend in the series. As soon as standard statistical tests are applied to ascertain whether or not the relationship should be attributed to chance, however, various problems arise. As noted above, the F-test (or, equivalently, the t-test for the regression weight) would lead one to conclude that the negative relationship between the number of UK drivers KSI and time is highly significant. These tests are based on the assumption that the errors are randomly distributed, an assumption that is clearly violated in this case.

When the first order residual autocorrelation (i.e. the residual autocorrelation for lag 1) is positive and significantly different from zero, a positive residual tends to be followed by one or more other positive residuals, and a negative residual tends to be followed by one or more other negative residuals. As pointed out in the literature (see, e.g., Ostrom, 1990; Belle, 2002), the error variance for standard statistical tests is seriously underestimated in this case. This in turn leads to a large overestimation of the F- or t-ratio, and therefore to overly optimistic conclusions about the linear relation between the dependent variable and time.

On the other hand, when the first order residual autocorrelation is negative and significantly deviates from zero, then a positive residual tends to be followed by a negative residual, and vice versa. In this case the error variance for the standard statistical test is seriously overestimated, leading to a large underestimation of the F- or t-ratio. Therefore, overly pessimistic conclusions about the linear relationship between the criterion variable and time will be drawn.

Time series analysis has the primary task to uncover the dynamic evolution of observations measured over time. It is assumed that the dynamic properties cannot be observed directly from the data. The unobserved dynamic process at time t is referred to as the *state* of the time series. The state of a time series may consist of several components, which will be introduced one by one in the following chapters. First, in Chapters 2, 3, and 4, components are presented that are useful for obtaining an adequate *description* of a time series. These components are the level, the slope and the seasonal. Then, in Chapters 5 and 6, components of the state are discussed that are helpful in finding *explanations* for the underlying development in the series. These components are explanatory and intervention variables. In Chapter 7 analyses are presented where descriptive and explanatory components from the previous chapters are combined into one model.

A third important application of time series analysis is the ability to *predict* or *forecast* (unknown) time series observations in the future. This aspect of time series analysis is discussed in Chapter 8. This chapter also presents a general notation for univariate state space models and alternative ways of dealing with explanatory and intervention variables. Further, confidence intervals, the filtered state, one-step ahead prediction errors and their variances, diagnostic tests, and the handling of missing observations in state space methods are discussed in this chapter. Chapter 9 introduces multivariate analysis of time series data. In Chapter 10 a very basic introduction to Box–Jenkins ARIMA models is provided, thus allowing for an evaluation of the relative merits of state space and Box–Jenkins methods for time series analysis. Finally, Chapter 11 shows how to perform all time series analyses discussed in Chapters 1 through 9 in SsfPack, a set of C routines collected in a library which has been linked to the Ox programming language.

Throughout the book, all univariate state space models are applied to the log of the monthly number of drivers killed or seriously injured (KSI) in the UK in the period January 1969 to December 1984 (see Figure 1.2). The actual numbers in this series (not in logs) are given in Appendix A. This is done even when the model under discussion is clearly not appropriate for this time series. In those cases, however, alternative illustrations are provided for which the model is closer to a correctly specified model. Moreover, in Chapters 4 and 7 results are presented of the analysis of quarterly price changes in the UK in the years 1950 through 2001.

Finally, most state space models are presented in their deterministic as well as in their stochastic form. What we mean by this distinction will become clear in the following chapters. The purpose of discussing the results of analyses with deterministic as well as with stochastic state space models is twofold. First, it shows the great flexibility of state space models in that both simple and multiple classical regression models are easily fitted in the framework of state space modelling. Second, it provides a means to offset the time series models presented in this book against classical regression analysis, showing the effectiveness of state space methods when dealing with time series data.

In the next chapter, we start off with a state space model that is even more simple than classical linear regression. In this model only the intercept of (1.1) is taken into consideration.

2

The local level model

A basic example of the state space model is the local level model. In this model the *level* component is allowed to vary in time. The level component can be conceived of as the equivalent of the intercept *a* in the classical regression model (1.1). As the intercept determines the level of the regression line, the level component plays the same role in state space modelling. The important difference is that the intercept in a regression model is fixed whereas the level component in a state space model is allowed to change from time point to time point. In case the level component does not change over time and is fixed for all time points, the level component is equivalent to the intercept. In other words, it is then a global level and applicable for all time points. In case the level component changes over time, the level component applies locally and therefore the corresponding model is referred to as the local level model.

The local level model can be formulated as

$$
\begin{aligned}
y_t &= \mu_t + \varepsilon_t, & \varepsilon_t &\sim \text{NID}(0, \sigma_\varepsilon^2) \\
\mu_{t+1} &= \mu_t + \xi_t, & \xi_t &\sim \text{NID}(0, \sigma_\xi^2)
\end{aligned}
\tag{2.1}
$$

for $t = 1, \ldots, n$, where μ_t is the unobserved level at time t, ε_t is the observation disturbance at time t, and ξ_t is what is called the level disturbance at time t. In the literature on state space models, the observation disturbances ε_t are also referred to as the *irregular component*. The observation and level disturbances are all assumed to be serially and mutually independent and normally distributed with zero mean and variances σ_ε^2 and σ_ξ^2, respectively. The first equation in (2.1) is called the *observation* or *measurement* equation, while the second equation is called the *state* equation. Since the level equation in (2.1) defines a *random walk* (see Chapter 10), the local level model is also referred to as the *random walk plus noise* model (where the noise refers to the irregular component).

The second equation in (2.1) is crucial in time series analysis. In the state equation, time dependencies in the observed time series are dealt with by letting the state at time $t + 1$ be a function of the state at time t. Therefore, it takes into account that the observed value of the series at time point $t + 1$ is usually more similar to the observed value of the time series at time point t than to any other previous value in the series.

When the state disturbances are all fixed on $\xi_t = 0$ for $t = 1, \ldots, n$, model (2.1) reduces to a *deterministic* model: in this case the level does not vary over time. On the other hand, when the level is allowed to vary over time, it is treated as a *stochastic* process. In Section 2.1 we discuss the results of the analysis of the log of the number of UK drivers KSI with a deterministic level. Then in Section 2.2, the latter results are compared with those obtained with a stochastic level component. As the local level model is not appropriate for the UK drivers KSI series, the model is also applied to the annual numbers of road traffic fatalities in Norway in Section 2.3.

2.1. Deterministic level

If the level disturbances in (2.1) are all fixed on $\xi_t = 0$ for $t = 1, \ldots, n$, it is easily verified that:

$$\text{for } t = 1: \qquad y_1 = \mu_1 + \varepsilon_1,$$

$$\mu_2 = \mu_1 + \xi_1 = \mu_1 + 0 = \mu_1$$

$$\text{for } t = 2: \qquad y_2 = \mu_2 + \varepsilon_2 = \mu_1 + \varepsilon_2,$$

$$\mu_3 = \mu_2 + \xi_2 = \mu_2 + 0 = \mu_1$$

$$\text{for } t = 3: \qquad y_3 = \mu_3 + \varepsilon_3 = \mu_1 + \varepsilon_3,$$

$$\mu_4 = \mu_3 + \xi_3 = \mu_3 + 0 = \mu_1$$

and so on.

Summarising, in this case the local level model (2.1) simplifies to

$$y_t = \mu_1 + \varepsilon_t, \qquad \varepsilon_t \sim \text{NID}(0, \sigma_\varepsilon^2) \tag{2.2}$$

for $t = 1, \ldots, n$. Therefore, in this special situation everything relies on the value of μ_1, the value of the level at time $t = 1$. Once this value is established, it remains constant for all other time points $t = 2, \ldots, n$.

Generally, in state space models the value of the unobserved state at the beginning of the time series (i.e. at $t = 1$) is unknown. There are two ways to deal with this problem. Either the researcher provides the first value, based on theoretical considerations, or some previous research, for example. Or this first value is *estimated* by a procedure that falls within the class of state space methods. Since nothing is usually known about the initial value of the state, the second approach is usually followed in practice, and will be used in all further analyses discussed in the present book. In state space modelling, the second approach is called *diffuse initialisation*.

In classical regression analysis the unknown parameters are the intercept and the regression coefficients, for which estimates can be obtained analytically. In state space methods the unknown parameters include the observation and state disturbance variances. These latter parameters are also known as *hyperparameters*. Unlike classical regression analysis, when a state space model contains two or more hyperparameters (i.e. disturbance variances) the (maximum likelihood) estimation of these hyperparameters requires an iterative procedure. The iterations aim to maximise the likelihood value with respect to the hyperparameters (see also Chapter 11). Numerical optimisation methods are employed for this task and they are based on an iterative search process to find the maximum in a numerically efficient way.

Since the variance of the level disturbances σ_ξ^2 is fixed at zero, only two parameters need to be estimated in model (2.2). These two parameters are μ_1 and σ_ε^2. Using the diffuse initialisation method, the analysis of the log of the number of UK drivers KSI with the deterministic level model yields the following results:

```
it0    f=    0.3297597 df=9.731e-007 e1=2.690e-006 e2=3.521e-008
Strong convergence
```

This output reflects the numerical search procedure where it0 refers to the initialisation step, f is the logged likelihood value for the hyperparameter value considered at iteration 0 whereas df is the first derivative of the likelihood function with respect to the hyperparameter and evaluated at the value of the hyperparameter at iteration 0. The values e1 and e2 indicate other measures of convergence of the maximisation procedure. In the numerical maximisation of the likelihood function, no iterations are required for the estimation of the parameters of the deterministic level model. This is in agreement with the fact that the parameter estimates of classical linear regression models can be determined analytically. The

11

value of the log-likelihood function that is maximised in state space methods is 0.3297597. The maximum likelihood estimate of the variance of the observation disturbances is $\hat{\sigma}_\varepsilon^2 = 0.029353$, and the maximum likelihood estimate of the level for $t = 1$ is $\hat{\mu}_1 = 7.4061$. The resulting equation for model (2.2) is

$$y_t = 7.4061 + \varepsilon_t.$$

Now, the sum of the log of the monthly number of UK drivers KSI in the period 1969–1984 happens to be 1421.97. Since

$$\bar{y} = \frac{1}{n} \sum_{t=1}^{n} y_t = \frac{1}{192} 1421.97 = 7.4061$$

for this time series, and

$$s_y^2 = \frac{1}{n-1} \sum_{t=1}^{n} (y_t - \bar{y})^2 = 0.029353,$$

this extremely simple state space model actually computes the mean and variance of the observed time series.

Thus, the best fitting decomposition based on model (2.2) is

$$y_t = \bar{y} + (y_t - \bar{y}). \tag{2.3}$$

This is not surprising, since it is well known that the best estimate for the parameter μ minimising the least-squares function

$$f(\mu) = \sum_{t=1}^{n} (y_t - \mu)^2$$

equals

$$\hat{\mu} = \frac{1}{n} \sum_{t=1}^{n} y_t,$$

the mean of variable y.

The level for model (2.2) is displayed in Figure 2.1, together with the observed time series. As the figure illustrates, the deterministic level is indeed a constant and does not vary over time as a result. Figure 2.2 contains a plot of the observation disturbances ε_t corresponding to the deterministic level model. Just as in the classical regression analysis discussed in Chapter 1, the disturbances ε_t of the deterministic level model are not randomly distributed in this case, and follow a very systematic pattern. In fact, the irregular component in Figure 2.2 simply consists

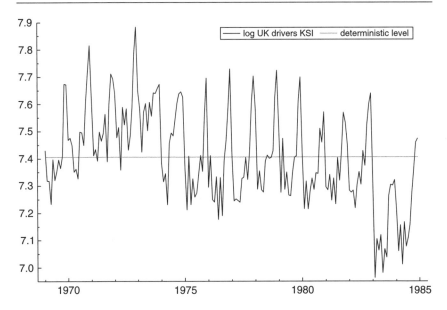

Figure 2.1. Deterministic level.

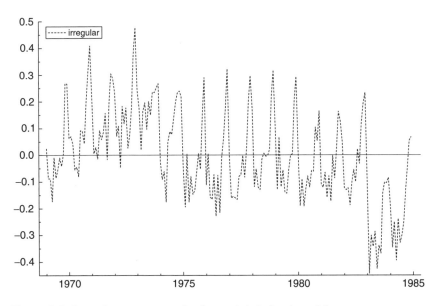

Figure 2.2. Irregular component for deterministic level model.

13

Table 2.1. Diagnostic tests for deterministic level model and log UK drivers KSI.

	statistic	value	critical value	assumption satisfied
independence	$Q(15)$	415.210	25.00	−
	$r(1)$	0.699	±0.14	−
	$r(12)$	0.677	±0.14	−
homoscedasticity	$H(64)$	2.058	1.67	−
normality	N	0.733	5.99	+

of the deviations of the observed time series from its mean, as already implied by (2.3).

Diagnostic tests for the assumptions of independence, homoscedasticity, and normality of the residuals of the analysis are presented in Table 2.1. A discussion of the exact definition, computation and interpretation of these diagnostic tests is postponed until Section 8.5. Even without this knowledge, however, it is easily seen that the values of the autocorrelations at lags 1 and 12 (see also Chapter 1), which are $r(1) = 0.699$ and $r(12) = 0.677$, respectively, both far exceed the 95% confidence limits of $\pm 2/\sqrt{n} = \pm 0.144$ for this time series with $n = 192$ observations.

The high amount of dependency between the residuals is confirmed by the very large value of the Q-test in Table 2.1. The Q-statistic is a general omnibus test that can be used to check whether the combined first k (in this case 15) autocorrelations in the correlogram deviate from zero. Since $Q(15) = 415.210$ and because this value is much larger than $\chi^2_{(15;0.05)} = 25.00$ (see Table 2.1), evaluated as a whole the first 15 autocorrelations significantly deviate from zero, meaning that the null hypothesis of independence must be rejected.

The H-statistic in Table 2.1 tests whether the variances of two consecutive and equal parts of the residuals are equal to one another. In the present case, the test shows that the variance of the first 64 elements of the residuals is unequal to the variance of the last 64 elements of the residuals, because $H(64) = 2.058$ is larger than the critical value of $F_{(64,64;0.025)} \approx 1.67$. This means that the assumption of homoscedasticity of the residuals is also not satisfied in the present analysis.

Finally, the N-statistic in Table 2.1 tests whether the skewness and kurtosis of the distribution of the residuals comply with a normal or Gaussian distribution. Since $N = 0.733$ is smaller than the critical value of $\chi^2_{(2;0.05)} = 5.99$ (see Table 2.1), the null hypothesis of normally distributed residuals is not rejected.

Summarising, the residuals of the deterministic level model neither satisfy the assumption of independence nor that of homoscedasticity; only the assumption of normality is not violated.

In order to compare the different state space models illustrated in the present book, throughout the Akaike Information Criterion (AIC) will be used:

$$\text{AIC} = \frac{1}{n}\left[-2n\log L_d + 2(q+w)\right],$$

where n is the number of observations in the time series, $\log L_d$ is the value of the diffuse log-likelihood function which is maximised in state space modelling, q is the number of diffuse initial values in the state, and w is the total number of disturbance variances estimated in the analysis. When comparing different models with the AIC the following rule holds: smaller values denote better fitting models than larger ones. A very useful property of this criterion is that it compensates for the number of estimated parameters in a model, thus allowing for a fair comparison between models involving different numbers of parameters. In the deterministic level model only one variance is estimated (σ_ε^2), and one initial value (μ_1). Therefore, the Akaike information criterion for the analysis of the log of the number of drivers KSI with the deterministic level model equals

$$\text{AIC} = \frac{1}{192}\left[-2(192)(0.3297597) + 2(1+1)\right] = -0.638686.$$

In the following sections, this value will be used for purposes of comparison with other state space models.

2.2. Stochastic level

When the level μ_t in model (2.1) is allowed to vary over time, on the other hand, the following results are obtained when estimating the hyperparameters by the method of maximum likelihood.

```
it0    f=    0.5673434 df=    0.08018 e1=    0.2550 e2=  0.003223
it1    f=    0.5799665 df=    0.1032 e1=    0.3199 e2=   0.3542
it2    f=    0.6404443 df=    0.08408 e1=    0.2048 e2=   0.02733
it3    f=    0.6424964 df=    0.03334 e1=    0.1025 e2=  0.003279
it4    f=    0.6429869 df=    0.02961 e1=   0.09162 e2= 0.0006207
it5    f=    0.6449777 df=   0.006552 e1=    0.02114 e2=  0.004098
it6    f=    0.6451632 df=   0.002400 e1=  0.007856 e2=  0.001422
it7    f=    0.6451949 df= 0.0004676 e1=  0.001543 e2= 0.0007765
it8    f=    0.6451960 df=3.338e-005 e1= 0.0001103 e2= 0.0001597
it9    f=    0.6451960 df=3.557e-006 e1=8.776e-006 e2=1.508e-005
Strong convergence
```

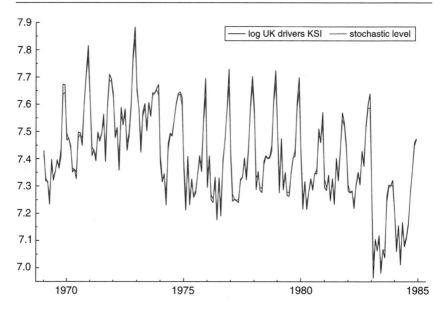

Figure 2.3. Stochastic level.

The algorithm converges in nine iterations. At convergence the value of the log-likelihood function is 0.6451960. The maximum likelihood estimate of the variance of the irregular component is $\widehat{\sigma}_\varepsilon^2 = 0.00222157$ and of the level disturbance variance is $\widehat{\sigma}_\xi^2 = 0.011866$. The maximum likelihood estimate of the initial value of the level at time point $t = 1$ is $\widehat{\mu}_1 = 7.4150$.

The stochastic level is illustrated in Figure 2.3, together with the observed time series. It shows that the observed time series is recovered quite well when the level is allowed to vary over time. It is nevertheless questionable whether the local level is appropriate for describing all the dynamics in the time series y_t.

Figure 2.4 contains a plot of the irregular component for this analysis. In this figure, the systematic pattern that was found in the residuals of the previous analysis is absent, and the observation disturbances seem to be much closer to independent random values, or – as is also said in control engineering where state space methods originated – to *white noise*.

To some extent, this is confirmed by the diagnostic tests of the residuals given in Table 2.2. The autocorrelation at lag 1 no longer deviates from zero, and the value of the overall Q-test for independence is much smaller than in the previous analysis. The test for heteroscedasticity is also no longer significant. However, both the values of $r(12)$ (the autocorrelation

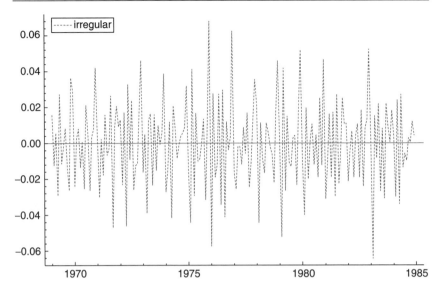

Figure 2.4. Irregular component for local level model.

at lag 12) and of the general Q-test still indicate significant serial correlation in the residuals. Moreover, according to Table 2.2 the residuals of the local level model do not satisfy the assumption of normality.

In the stochastic level model two variances are estimated (σ_ε^2 and σ_ξ^2), and one diffuse element (μ_1). Therefore, the Akaike information criterion for this analysis equals

$$\text{AIC} = \frac{1}{192} \left[-2(192)(0.6451960) + 2(1+2) \right] = -1.25914.$$

This value is much smaller than for the deterministic level model, meaning that the stochastic level model fits the data better.

In conclusion, the stochastic level model appears to be an improvement upon the deterministic level model. A lot of the dependencies between the observation disturbances in Figure 2.2 have disappeared in Figure 2.4.

Table 2.2. Diagnostic tests for local level model and log UK drivers KSI.

	statistic	value	critical value	assumption satisfied
independence	$Q(15)$	105.390	23.68	−
	$r(1)$	0.009	±0.14	+
	$r(12)$	0.537	±0.14	−
homoscedasticity	$H(64)$	1.064	1.67	+
normality	N	13.242	5.99	−

Moreover, the Akaike information criterion indicates that the stochastic level model yields a better representation of the time series than the deterministic level model. However, the diagnostic tests in Table 2.2 also reveal that the stochastic level model is by no means the appropriate model for describing the time series at hand, as will become clearer in Chapter 4. In the next section, therefore, an analysis is presented where the local level model provides a more adequate description of the data.

2.3. The local level model and Norwegian fatalities

Applying the local level model to the log of the annual number of road traffic fatalities in Norway as observed for the 34 years of 1970 through to 2003 (see Appendix B and Figure 2.5), the following results are obtained.

```
it0    f=    0.7755299 df=    0.1692 e1=    0.5779 e2= 0.006216
it1    f=    0.8205220 df=    0.1248 e1=    0.4053 e2= 0.009750
it2    f=    0.8464841 df=    0.02166 e1=   0.06664 e2=  0.01080
it3    f=    0.8468295 df=  0.005806 e1=   0.01800 e2= 0.0007435
it4    f=    0.8468620 df= 0.0003182 e1= 0.0009326 e2= 0.0003626
it5    f=    0.8468622 df=1.945e-005 e1=5.699e-005 e2=2.894e-005
Strong convergence
```

At convergence the value of the log-likelihood function is 0.8468622. The maximum likelihood estimate of the irregular variance is $\hat{\sigma}_\varepsilon^2 = 0.00326838$,

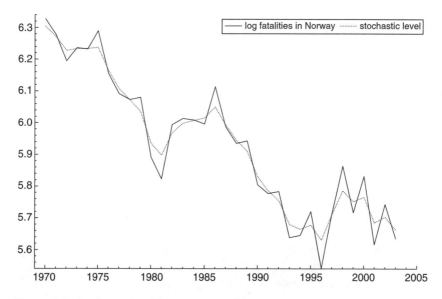

Figure 2.5. Stochastic level for Norwegian fatalities.

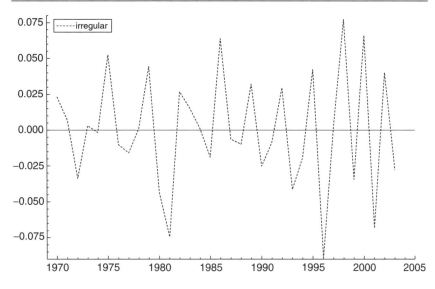

Figure 2.6. Irregular component for Norwegian fatalities.

while the maximum likelihood estimate of the variance of the level disturbances equals $\widehat{\sigma}_\xi^2 = 0.0047026$. The maximum likelihood estimate of the
initial value of the level at time point $t = 1$ is $\widehat{\mu}_1 = 6.3048$. The stochastic
level is illustrated in Figure 2.5, together with the observed time series.

Figure 2.6 contains a plot of the irregular component. The diagnostic
tests for independence, homoscedasticity, and normality of the residuals
of this analysis are given in Table 2.3. The autocorrelations at lags 1 and
4 are well within the 95% confidence limits of $\pm 2/\sqrt{n} = \pm 0.343$ for this
time series. Moreover, since $Q(10) < \chi^2_{(9;0.05)}$, $H(11) < F_{(12,12;0.025)}$, and $N <$
$\chi^2_{(2;0.05)}$ (see also Section 8.5), these tests indicate that the residuals satisfy
all of the assumptions of the local level model (2.1).

Table 2.3. Diagnostic tests for local level model and log Norwegian
fatalities.

	statistic	value	critical value	assumption satisfied
independence	$Q(10)$	6.228	16.92	+
	$r(1)$	−0.127	±0.34	+
	$r(4)$	−0.105	±0.34	+
homoscedasticity	$H(11)$	1.746	3.28	+
normality	N	1.191	5.99	+

The value of the Akaike information criterion for this analysis equals

$$\text{AIC} = \frac{1}{34}\left[-2(34)(0.8468622) + 2(1+2)\right] = -1.51725,$$

which is a great improvement upon the deterministic level model applied to these data, since the AIC value for the deterministic model equals 0.040245. Adding a slope component (see Chapter 3) to model (2.1) does not improve the description of this time series, as this results in an AIC value of only -1.28035.

3

The local linear trend model

The local linear trend model is obtained by adding a *slope component* v_t to the local level model, as follows:

$$
\begin{aligned}
y_t &= \mu_t + \varepsilon_t, & \varepsilon_t &\sim \text{NID}(0, \sigma_\varepsilon^2) \\
\mu_{t+1} &= \mu_t + v_t + \xi_t, & \xi_t &\sim \text{NID}(0, \sigma_\xi^2) \\
v_{t+1} &= v_t + \zeta_t, & \zeta_t &\sim \text{NID}(0, \sigma_\zeta^2)
\end{aligned}
\tag{3.1}
$$

for $t = 1, \ldots, n$. The local linear trend model contains two state equations: one for modelling the level, and one for modelling the slope. The slope v_t in (3.1) can be conceived of as the equivalent of the regression coefficient b in classical regression model (1.1). The value of b determines the angle of the regression line with the x-axis. For the local linear trend model, the slope also determines the angle of the trend line with the x-axis. Again, the important difference is that the regression coefficient or weight b is fixed in classical regression, whereas the slope in (3.1) is allowed to change over time. In the literature on time series analysis the slope is also referred to as the *drift*.

First the results of the analysis of the UK drivers KSI with the deterministic linear trend model are presented in Section 3.1. Then in Section 3.2, the latter results are compared with those obtained with the stochastic linear trend model. Since the local linear trend model is still not the correct model for describing this time series, Section 3.4 presents the results of an analysis of the annual numbers of road traffic fatalities in Finland with the local linear trend model.

3.1. Deterministic level and slope

Fixing all state disturbances ξ_t and ζ_t in (3.1) on zero, it is easily verified that

21

for $t = 1$:
$$y_1 = \mu_1 + \varepsilon_1,$$
$$\mu_2 = \mu_1 + \nu_1 + \xi_1 = \mu_1 + \nu_1 + 0 = \mu_1 + \nu_1$$
$$\nu_2 = \nu_1 + \zeta_1 = \nu_1 + 0 = \nu_1$$

for $t = 2$:
$$y_2 = \mu_2 + \varepsilon_2 = \mu_1 + \nu_1 + \varepsilon_2,$$
$$\mu_3 = \mu_2 + \nu_2 + \xi_2 = \mu_1 + 2\nu_1 + 0 = \mu_1 + 2\nu_1$$
$$\nu_3 = \nu_2 + \zeta_2 = \nu_1 + 0 = \nu_1$$

for $t = 3$:
$$y_3 = \mu_3 + \varepsilon_3 = \mu_1 + 2\nu_1 + \varepsilon_3,$$
$$\mu_4 = \mu_3 + \nu_3 + \xi_3 = \mu_1 + 3\nu_1 + 0 = \mu_1 + 3\nu_1$$
$$\nu_4 = \nu_3 + \zeta_3 = \nu_1 + 0 = \nu_1$$

and so on.

Therefore, in this case the linear trend model simplifies to

$$y_t = \mu_1 + \nu_1 g_t + \varepsilon_t, \qquad \varepsilon_t \sim \mathrm{NID}(0, \sigma_\varepsilon^2)$$

for $t = 1, \ldots, n$, where the predictor variable $g_t = t - 1$ for $t = 1, \ldots, n$ is effectively time, and μ_1 and ν_1 are the initial values of the level and the slope. The latter equation can also be written as

$$y_t = (\mu_1 - \nu_1) + \nu_1 (g_t + 1) + \varepsilon_t$$
$$\qquad\qquad\qquad\qquad \varepsilon_t \sim \mathrm{NID}(0, \sigma_\varepsilon^2) \qquad (3.2)$$
$$= (\mu_1 - \nu_1) + \nu_1 x_t + \varepsilon_t$$

with $x_t = g_t + 1 = t = 1, 2, \ldots, n$.

The analysis of the log of the number of UK drivers KSI series using diffuse initialisation of the unknown values for μ_1 and ν_1 yields the following results:

```
it0    f=     0.4140728 df=1.297e-006 e1=3.742e-006 e2=4.492e-008
Strong convergence
```

Again, no iterations are required for the estimation of the parameters of this deterministic model. The value of the log-likelihood function is 0.4140728. The maximum likelihood estimate of the variance of the irregular is $\widehat{\sigma}_\varepsilon^2 = 0.022998$. The maximum likelihood estimates of the level and the slope at $t = 1$ are $\widehat{\mu}_1 = 7.5444$ and $\widehat{\nu}_1 = -0.0014480$, respectively. Substituting the latter values in (3.2) yields

$$y_t = 7.5458 - 0.00145 x_t + \varepsilon_t,$$

Table 3.1. Diagnostic tests for deterministic linear trend model and log UK drivers KSI.

	statistic	value	critical value	assumption satisfied
independence	$Q(15)$	305.680	25.00	−
	$r(1)$	0.610	±0.14	−
	$r(12)$	0.631	±0.14	−
homoscedasticity	$H(63)$	1.360	1.67	+
normality	N	1.790	5.99	+

for $t = 1, \ldots, n$ and $x_t = t$, with residual error variance $\hat{\sigma}_\varepsilon^2 = 0.022998$, which is identical to the classical regression equation discussed in Chapter 1.

The linear trend (consisting of level plus slope) for the deterministic linear trend model is therefore identical to the regression line displayed in Figure 1.1, and the irregular for this analysis is identical to the one shown in Figure 1.3.

The results of the diagnostic tests for the residuals of the analysis are given in Table 3.1. The tests for homoscedasticity and normality are satisfactory, but the most important assumption of independence is clearly violated in this analysis.

Since one variance is estimated in model (3.2) together with two initial elements (i.e., μ_1 and ν_1), the Akaike information criterion for this model equals

$$\mathrm{AIC} = \frac{1}{192}\left[-2(192)(0.4140728) + 2(2+1)\right] = -0.796896.$$

The deterministic linear trend model (3.2) therefore yields a better fit for the log of the number of UK drivers KSI series than the deterministic level model (see Section 2.1). However, the fit of the model is not as good as that obtained with the stochastic level model (see Section 2.2).

3.2. Stochastic level and slope

Allowing both the level and the slope to vary over time in model (3.1), the following results are obtained:

```
it0    f=   0.4839008 df=   0.04716 e1=    0.1279 e2=  0.001858
it5    f=   0.5260923 df=   0.07616 e1=    0.2568 e2=  0.005020
it10   f=   0.6215185 df=   0.01589 e1=   0.03640 e2=  0.008347
it15   f=   0.6236505 df=  0.007679 e1=   0.02624 e2=  0.002837
it20   f=   0.6247839 df=  0.002160 e1=  0.004991 e2=  0.009222
it23   f=   0.6247935 df=2.575e-006 e1=5.967e-006 e2=5.852e-006
Strong convergence
```

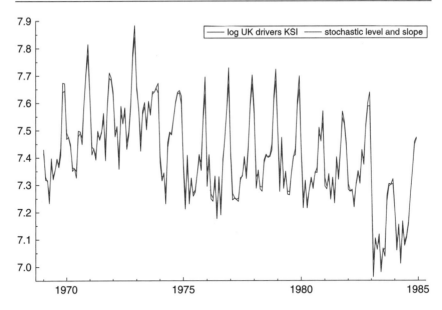

Figure 3.1. Trend of stochastic linear trend model.

At convergence the value of the log-likelihood function equals 0.6247935. The maximum likelihood estimate of the variance of the irregular is $\widehat{\sigma}_\varepsilon^2 = 0.0021181$, and the maximum likelihood estimates of the state disturbance variances are $\widehat{\sigma}_\xi^2 = 0.012128$ and $\widehat{\sigma}_\zeta^2 = 1.5E^{-}11$, respectively. The maximum likelihood estimates of the initial values of the level and the slope are $\widehat{\mu}_1 = 7.4157$ and $\widehat{v}_1 = 0.00028896$, respectively. The state variance for the slope component is almost equal to zero, meaning that the value of the slope hardly changes over time.

The trend (consisting of level plus slope) for the stochastic linear trend model (3.1) is displayed in Figure 3.1, while Figure 3.2 contains the separate development of the slope over time. It may seem that the change of the slope over time is considerable in Figure 3.2, but when the scale on the y-axis is taken into consideration (in relation to the variation in y), it is clear that the slope is effectively constant. This is consistent with the close-to-zero disturbance variance for this component.

The irregular component for model (3.1) is displayed in Figure 3.3. The systematic pattern in the irregular of the deterministic linear trend model as observed in Figure 1.3 has largely disappeared in Figure 3.3. The values of the diagnostic tests for the residuals of the analysis are given in Table 3.2. In contrast with the previous analysis, the first autocorrelation in the correlogram ($r(1)$) is close to zero but the autocorrelation at lag 12 is

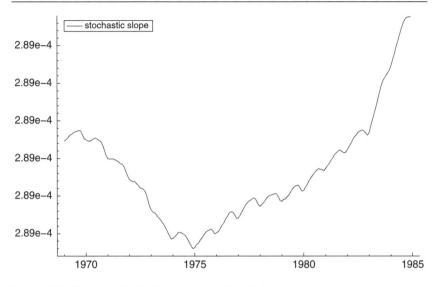

Figure 3.2. Slope of stochastic linear trend model.

still too large. The overall Q-test for the first 15 autocorrelations confirms that the assumption of independence is still not satisfied. The test for homoscedasticity is satisfactory, but here the assumption of normality is clearly violated.

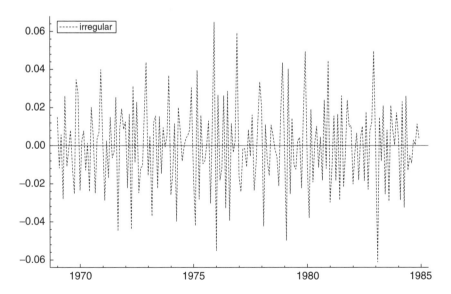

Figure 3.3. Irregular component of stochastic linear trend model.

25

Table 3.2. Diagnostic tests for the local linear trend model applied to the log of the UK drivers KSI.

	statistic	value	critical value	assumption satisfied
independence	$Q(15)$	100.610	22.36	−
	$r(1)$	0.005	±0.14	+
	$r(12)$	0.532	±0.14	−
homoscedasticity	$H(63)$	1.058	1.67	+
normality	N	14.946	5.99	−

The Akaike information criterion for the stochastic linear trend model equals

$$\text{AIC} = \frac{1}{192}\left[-2(192)(0.6247935) + 2(2+3)\right] = -1.1975.$$

For the log of the UK drivers KSI series the fit of the local linear trend model is inferior to that obtained with the local level model (see Section 2.2), but clearly superior to the fit obtained with a classical linear regression analysis (as modelled by the deterministic linear trend model). This suggests that the inclusion of a stochastic slope has not helped the analysis in this case.

3.3. Stochastic level and deterministic slope

Another possibility is to consider model (3.1) where only the level is allowed to vary over time whereas the slope is treated deterministically. In this case it is not very difficult to verify that model (3.1) can written as

$$y_t = \mu_t + \varepsilon_t, \qquad \varepsilon_t \sim \text{NID}(0, \sigma_\varepsilon^2)$$
$$\mu_{t+1} = \mu_t + \nu_1 + \xi_t, \quad \xi_t \sim \text{NID}(0, \sigma_\xi^2)$$

$$(3.3)$$

for $t = 1, \ldots, n$. The analysis of the log of the UK drivers KSI with model (3.3) yields the following results:

```
it0    f=    0.5432387 df=    0.08367 e1=    0.2659 e2=  0.003367
it1    f=    0.5569736 df=    0.1072 e1=    0.3318 e2=    0.3264
it2    f=    0.6210248 df=    0.05154 e1=    0.1278 e2=    0.02498
it3    f=    0.6215160 df=    0.03132 e1=    0.09584 e2=  0.002430
it4    f=    0.6224598 df=    0.02822 e1=    0.08747 e2=  0.001277
it5    f=    0.6241177 df=    0.02014 e1=    0.04977 e2=  0.003469
it6    f=    0.6246745 df=    0.007840 e1=    0.01932 e2=  0.001947
it7    f=    0.6247859 df=    0.001003 e1=    0.003322 e2=  0.001153
it8    f=    0.6247932 df= 0.0001671 e1= 0.0004376 e2=  0.0003907
it9    f=    0.6247935 df=1.173e-005 e1=2.880e-005 e2=8.883e-005
Strong convergence
```

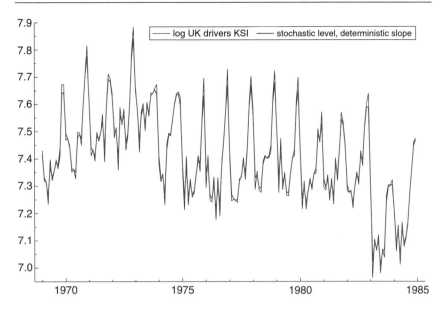

Figure 3.4. Trend of stochastic level and deterministic slope model.

At convergence the value of the log-likelihood function equals 0.6247935. The maximum likelihood estimate of the variance of the observation disturbances is $\hat{\sigma}_\varepsilon^2 = 0.00211869$, and the maximum likelihood estimate of the variance of the level disturbances is $\hat{\sigma}_\xi^2 = 0.0121271$. The maximum likelihood estimates of the values of the level and the slope right at the start of the series are $\hat{\mu}_1 = 7.4157$ and $\hat{\nu}_1 = 0.00028897$, respectively.

The trend (consisting of stochastic level and deterministic slope) is displayed in Figure 3.4. The deterministic slope is simply a constant, equal to $\hat{\nu}_1 = 0.00028897$ for $t = 1, \ldots, n$. The irregular component for this model is virtually identical to the one in Figure 3.3, and the results of the diagnostic tests on the residuals are virtually identical to those presented in Table 3.2.

The Akaike information criterion for the linear trend model with stochastic level and deterministic slope equals

$$\text{AIC} = \frac{1}{192}\left[-2(192)(0.6247935) + 2(2 + 2)\right] = -1.20792.$$

Thus, the AIC of this model is slightly better than the fit of the linear trend model with stochastic level and stochastic slope. However, it is still inferior to the AIC of the stochastic level model (see Section 2.2).

27

It follows that the value of the variance for the slope component is almost zero and it leads to an almost negligible fluctuation in the slope (see Figure 3.2). In state space modelling, a near zero state disturbance variance indicates that the corresponding state component may as well be treated as a deterministic effect, resulting in a more parsimonious model. Treating the slope component deterministically indeed yields a slightly better fitting model. However, the fit of the latter model is still inferior to the one obtained with the local level model. This means that the addition of a slope component to the local level model is not effective in improving the description of the observed time series. Therefore, the slope is a redundant component in this case, and is removed from further analyses of the UK drivers KSI series. A similar strategy is described by Ord and Young (2004) on the basis of *t*-statistics rather than the AIC.

As the diagnostic tests in Table 3.2 indicate, the local linear trend model is still not the appropriate model for obtaining a good description of the log of the UK drivers KSI, for reasons that will be explained in Chapter 4. In the next section we therefore discuss a time series for which the local linear trend model is more appropriate.

3.4. The local linear trend model and Finnish fatalities

In this section the local linear trend model is applied to the log of the annual numbers of road traffic fatalities in Finland as observed for the years 1970 through 2003 (see Appendix B and Figure 3.5). Allowing both the level and the slope component to vary over time, at convergence the value of the log-likelihood function equals 0.7864746. The value of the AIC for this analysis therefore equals

$$\text{AIC} = \frac{1}{34}\left[-2(34)(0.7864746) + 2(2+3)\right] = -1.27883.$$

The maximum likelihood estimates of the variances corresponding to the irregular, level, and slope components are $\hat{\sigma}_\varepsilon^2 = 0.00320083$, $\hat{\sigma}_\xi^2 = 9.69606E-26$, and $\hat{\sigma}_\zeta^2 = 0.00153314$, respectively.

Since the variance of the level disturbances is, for all practical purposes, equal to zero, the analysis is repeated with a deterministic level component, yielding the following results:

```
it0   f=   0.7544891 df=   0.07002 e1=   0.2599 e2=  0.002318
it1   f=   0.7735067 df=   0.05625 e1=   0.2050 e2=  0.003601
it2   f=   0.7858661 df=   0.01570 e1=  0.04919 e2=  0.003735
it3   f=   0.7864624 df=  0.002545 e1= 0.007951 e2= 0.0006039
```

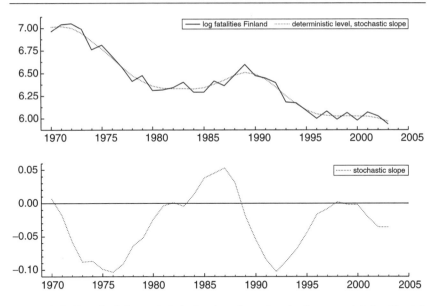

Figure 3.5. Trend of deterministic level and stochastic slope model for Finnish fatalities (top), and stochastic slope component (bottom).

```
it4    f=    0.7864746 df=4.601e-005 e1= 0.0001437 e2=6.199e-005
it5    f=    0.7864746 df=2.310e-005 e1=7.211e-005 e2=6.183e-007
Strong convergence
```

At convergence the value of the log-likelihood function equals 0.7864746. The maximum likelihood estimates of the variances of the observation and slope disturbances are $\widehat{\sigma}_\varepsilon^2 = 0.00320083$, and $\widehat{\sigma}_\zeta^2 = 0.00153314$, respectively. The maximum likelihood estimates of the values of the level and the slope at the start of the series are $\widehat{\mu}_1 = 7.0133$ and $\widehat{\nu}_1 = 0.0068482$.

The trend (consisting of a deterministic level and a stochastic slope) of this analysis is displayed at the top of Figure 3.5, while the stochastic slope is shown separately at the bottom of the figure. Since the time varying slope component in Figure 3.5 models the rate of change in the series, it can be interpreted as follows. When the slope component is *positive*, the trend in the series is *increasing*. Thus, the trend of fatalities in Finland was increasing in the years 1970, 1982, 1984 through to 1988, and in 1998 (see Figure 3.5). On the other hand, the trend is *decreasing* when the slope component is *negative*. The trend in the fatalities of Finland was therefore decreasing in the remaining years of the series.

Moreover, when the slope is positive and increasing, the increase becomes more pronounced, while the increase becomes less pronounced

The local linear trend model

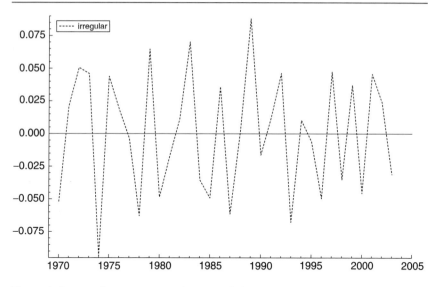

Figure 3.6. Irregular component for Finnish fatalities.

when the slope is positive but decreasing. Conversely, when the slope is negative and decreasing then the decrease becomes more pronounced, while the decrease levels off when the slope is negative but increasing.

The irregular component of the analysis is shown in Figure 3.6. The diagnostic tests for the residuals of the analysis are given in Table 3.3. Since $Q(10) < \chi^2_{(9;0.05)}$, $1/H(11) < F_{(12,12;0.025)}$, and $N < \chi^2_{(2;0.05)}$ (see also Section 8.5), the assumptions of independence, homoscedasticity, and normality are all satisfied, indicating that the deterministic level and stochastic slope model yields an appropriate description of the log of the annual traffic fatalities in Finland.

Table 3.3. Diagnostic tests for deterministic level and stochastic slope model, and log Finnish fatalities.

	statistic	value	critical value	assumption satisfied
independence	$Q(10)$	7.044	16.92	+
	$r(1)$	−0.028	±0.34	+
	$r(4)$	−0.094	±0.34	+
homoscedasticity	$1/H(11)$	1.348	3.28	+
normality	N	0.644	5.99	+

30

The Akaike information criterion for the deterministic level and stochastic slope model equals

$$\text{AIC} = \frac{1}{34} \left[-2(34)(0.7864746) + 2(2 + 2) \right] = -1.33766.$$

Thus, the fit of this model is slightly better than the fit of a model with stochastic level and stochastic slope. Since the log-likelihood values are identical for the two models, the improved fit of the second model can be completely attributed to its greater parsimony. The model with a deterministic level and stochastic slope is also called the *smooth trend* model, reflecting the fact that the trend of such a model is relatively smooth compared to a trend with a level disturbance variance different from zero.

As Section 3.1 illustrates, the deterministic linear trend model actually performs a classical regression analysis of time series observations on the predictor variable time. This is an important and very useful result. By way of the Akaike information criterion, it opens up the possibility of a straightforward, fair and quantitative assessment of the relative merits of state space methods and classical regression models when it comes to the analysis of time series data. The reverse is also true: the state space models discussed in the present book are regression models in which the parameters (intercept and regression coefficient(s)) are allowed to vary over time. State space models are therefore also sometimes referred to as *dynamic linear* models.

4

The local level model with seasonal

Most readers will probably have understood that an essential aspect of the UK drivers KSI series has been overlooked in the analyses discussed so far. The time series in Figure 1.2 has a yearly recurring pattern. The nature of this pattern becomes even more clear in Figure 4.1 where vertical lines separate each calendar year in the observed time series of Figure 1.2.

Inspecting the monthly development for each year in Figure 4.1, the following regularity emerges: more drivers are killed or seriously injured at the end of a year than in other periods of a year. In time series analysis, this recurring pattern is referred to as a *seasonal* effect. Whenever a time series consists of hourly, daily, monthly, or quarterly observations with respective periodicity of 24 (hours), 7 (days), 12 (months), or 4 (quarters), one should always be on the alert for possible seasonal effects in the series.

In a state space framework, the seasonal effect can be modelled by adding a seasonal component either to the local level model or to the local linear trend model. Since it was found in the previous chapter that the slope component is redundant in describing the time series in Figure 4.1, the investigation of the effect of adding a seasonal component will be restricted to the local level model. In the case of quarterly data, this takes the following form:

$$y_t = \mu_t + \gamma_t + \varepsilon_t, \qquad\qquad \varepsilon_t \sim \text{NID}(0, \sigma_\varepsilon^2)$$

$$\mu_{t+1} = \mu_t + \xi_t, \qquad\qquad \xi_t \sim \text{NID}(0, \sigma_\xi^2)$$

$$\gamma_{1,t+1} = -\gamma_{1,t} - \gamma_{2,t} - \gamma_{3,t} + \omega_t, \quad \omega_t \sim \text{NID}(0, \sigma_\omega^2) \qquad (4.1)$$

$$\gamma_{2,t+1} = \gamma_{1,t},$$

$$\gamma_{3,t+1} = \gamma_{2,t},$$

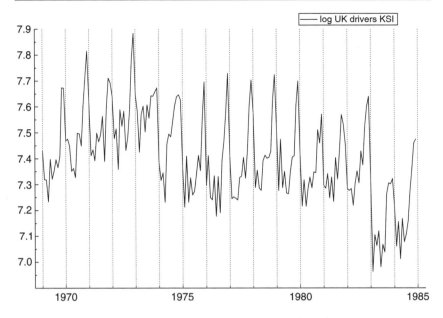

Figure 4.1. Log of number of UK drivers KSI with time lines for years.

for $t = 1, \ldots, n$, where $\gamma_t = \gamma_{1,t}$ denotes the seasonal component. The disturbances ω_t in (4.1) allow the seasonal to change over time. The initial values μ_1, $\gamma_{1,1}$, $\gamma_{2,1}$ and $\gamma_{3,1}$ are treated as fixed and unknown coefficients.

In contrast with the level and slope components, where each component requires one state equation, the seasonal component generally requires $(s - 1)$ state equations where s is given by the periodicity of the seasonal. For quarterly data (where we have $s = 4$), three state equations are needed, as is shown in (4.1). The fourth and fifth equations are identities which can be interpreted as follows. Define $\gamma_{i,t}$ as the ith quarter of time period t. Then the fourth equation tells you that the quarter of the next period $t + 1$ is the next quarter $i + 1$ from the current period t. Since this is a fact of life we cannot add disturbances to such identity equations! The third equation in (4.1) can also be written as

$$\gamma_{t+1} = -\gamma_t - \gamma_{t-1} - \gamma_{t-2} + \omega_t, \tag{4.2}$$

for $t = s - 1, \ldots, n$. We notice that the time index for (4.2) starts at $s - 1 = 3$. Since it follows from (4.1) that $\gamma_1 = \gamma_{1,1}$, $\gamma_2 = \gamma_{1,2} = \gamma_{2,1}$ and $\gamma_3 = \gamma_{1,3} = \gamma_{2,2} = \gamma_{3,1}$, we also treat γ_1, γ_2 and γ_3 as fixed and unknown coefficients. Given a set of values for $\{\gamma_1, \gamma_2, \gamma_3\}$, the recursion (4.2) is valid for $t = s - 1, \ldots, n$.

When the seasonal effect γ_t is not allowed to change over time, we require $\omega_t = 0$ for all $t = s - 1, \ldots, n$. This is achieved by setting $\sigma_\omega^2 = 0$. It follows that

$$\sum_{j=0}^{s-1} \gamma_{t-j} = 0, \tag{4.3}$$

for $t = s, \ldots, n$. When the seasonal is allowed to vary over time, that is $\sigma_\omega^2 > 0$, (4.3) is not satisfied due to the random increments of ω_t. However, the expectation of seasonal disturbance ω_t equals zero. As a result, the expectation of the sum $\gamma_t + \gamma_{t-1} + \ldots + \gamma_{t-s+1}$ also equals zero for $t = s, \ldots, n$.

Since the log of the number of UK drivers KSI in Figure 4.1 consists of monthly instead of quarterly data, the periodicity of the seasonal is $s = 12$, implying that the modelling of (4.1) requires a total of 12 state equations (one for the level and 11 for the seasonal). The seasonal specification in (4.1) is called a *dummy seasonal*. It may be noted that other specifications than the dummy seasonal can be used too. For example, the *trigonometric seasonal* can be considered. For details about such alternative specifications of the seasonal we refer to Durbin and Koopman (2001), as these are beyond the scope of the present book.

4.1. Deterministic level and seasonal

Fixing the level and seasonal disturbances ξ_t and ω_t in (4.1) to zero, the analysis of the time series in Figure 4.1 using diffuse initialisation of the values of the 12 state equations at $t = 1$ yields the following results:

```
it0    f=    0.4174873 df=1.613e-006 e1=4.871e-006 e2=5.340e-008
Strong convergence
```

As is the case for all completely deterministic models, the estimation process requires no iterations. At convergence the value of the log-likelihood function is 0.4174873. The maximum likelihood estimate of the variance of the observation disturbances is $\widehat{\sigma}_\varepsilon^2 = 0.0175885$. The maximum likelihood estimate of μ_1 is $\widehat{\mu}_1 = 7.4061$. Since the level is deterministic we have $\widehat{\mu}_t = \widehat{\mu}_1 = 7.4061$ for $t = 1, \ldots, n$. Therefore, the estimated deterministic level is again equal to the mean of the observed time series (see also Section 2.1). At this point, we refrain from giving the maximum likelihood estimates of the initial values of the 11 state equations required

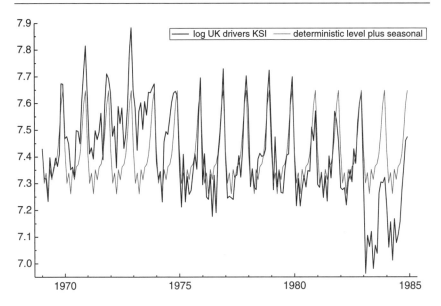

Figure 4.2. Combined deterministic level and seasonal.

for the modelling of the seasonal, because these are not very informative in the present context.

The combined deterministic level and seasonal are displayed in Figure 4.2, while these two components are plotted separately in Figures 4.3 and 4.4, respectively.

By denoting $\bar{y}$ as the overall mean of the log of the numbers of drivers KSI and $\bar{y}_j$ as the mean of the log of the numbers of drivers KSI for month j in the series ($j = 1, \ldots, s$), the deterministic level and seasonal model is given by

$$\hat{y}_t = \hat{\mu}_t + \hat{\gamma}_t = \bar{y} + (\bar{y}_j - \bar{y})$$

for $t = 1, \ldots, n$. Note that

$$\sum_{j=0}^{s-1} \hat{\gamma}_{t-j} = \sum_{j=1}^{s} (\bar{y}_j - \bar{y}) = 0,$$

from which it follows that the seasonal component satisfies (4.3). The deterministic level and seasonal model actually performs a one-way ANOVA with 12 treatment levels (see, e.g., Kirk, 1968). The F-test for the seasonal (with denominator $\hat{\sigma}_\varepsilon^2 = 0.0175885$) is $F_{(11,180)} = 12.614$ and this is very significant ($p < 0.01$). The F-test is based on the assumption of random errors. However, as Figure 4.5 clearly indicates, the observation

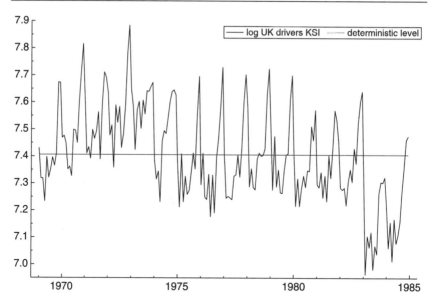

Figure 4.3. Deterministic level.

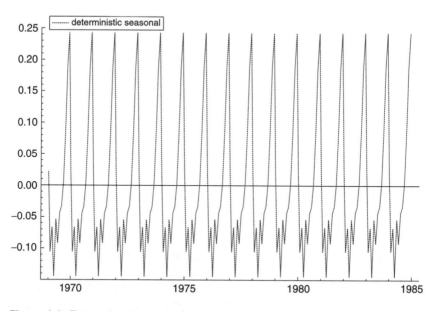

Figure 4.4. Deterministic seasonal.

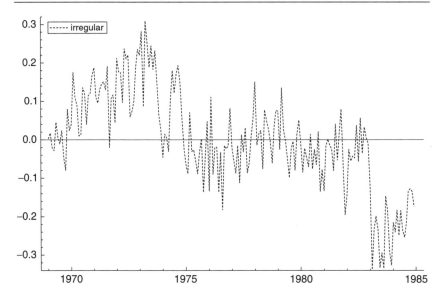

Figure 4.5. Irregular component for deterministic level and seasonal model.

disturbances of the deterministic level and seasonal model are not independently distributed, and the F-test is therefore seriously flawed.

This is confirmed by the results of the diagnostic tests in Table 4.1. They show that the residuals do not satisfy any of the assumptions, except for normality.

Since we are dealing with monthly data, model (4.1) contains 12 state equations for which 12 initial state values need to be estimated. Given the fact that in addition one variance is estimated for the deterministic level and seasonal model, the Akaike information criterion for this model equals

$$\text{AIC} = \frac{1}{192}\left[-2(192)(0.4174873) + 2(12 + 1)\right] = -0.699558.$$

Table 4.1. Diagnostic tests for deterministic level and seasonal model and log UK drivers KSI.

	statistic	value	critical value	assumption satisfied
independence	$Q(15)$	751.580	25.00	−
	$r(1)$	0.724	±0.14	−
	$r(12)$	0.431	±0.14	−
homoscedasticity	$H(60)$	3.400	1.67	−
normality	N	1.971	5.99	+

Therefore, the AIC of the deterministic level and seasonal model is, somewhat surprisingly, not as good as that of the deterministic linear trend model (-0.796896), although it is slightly better than the deterministic level model (-0.638686).

In the previous chapters it was found that deterministic state space models are identical to some form of classical regression analysis. This suggests that the deterministic level and seasonal model must also have its counterpart in classical regression analysis. The question is: which classical regression model is involved here? Results identical to the deterministic level and seasonal model presented above are obtained by performing the following classical multiple regression analysis.

Eleven variables are constructed according to the following recipe. The first variable is given the value 11 (i.e. $s - 1$) whenever an observation in the time series falls in the month of January, and minus one for all the other months of the year. The second variable is set equal to 11 whenever an observation in the time series falls in the month of February and minus one elsewhere. And so on, until the eleventh and last variable. This last variable is given the value 11 for the month of November and minus one elsewhere. A classical multiple regression analysis with an intercept variable together with these 11 'dummy' variables against the log of UK drivers KSI, yields an estimate of the intercept identical to the level shown in Figure 4.3, while the sum of the 11 dummy variables weighted by their respective regression coefficients is identical to the seasonal in Figure 4.4. The overal sum of the seasonal effect in one year is obviously equal to zero.

4.2. Stochastic level and seasonal

The level and the seasonal in (4.1) can be allowed to vary over time. In that case, the following results are obtained:

```
it0     f=     0.6967041 df=    0.1701 e1=    0.7878 e2= 0.003672
it5     f=     0.8803781 df=    0.08417 e1=   0.4735 e2= 0.002996
it10    f=     0.9353563 df=    0.01276 e1=   0.04076 e2= 0.001999
it15    f=     0.9369055 df= 0.0002212 e1= 0.0007954 e2= 0.0001283
it18    f=     0.9369063 df=6.131e-006 e1=1.809e-005 e2=8.189e-006
Strong convergence
```

At convergence the value of the log-likelihood function is 0.9369063. The maximum likelihood estimate of the irregular variance is $\hat{\sigma}_\varepsilon^2 = 0.00341592$ and the maximum likelihood estimates of the state variances are given by $\hat{\sigma}_\xi^2 = 0.000935947$ and $\hat{\sigma}_\omega^2 = 0.00000050$, respectively. Plots of the

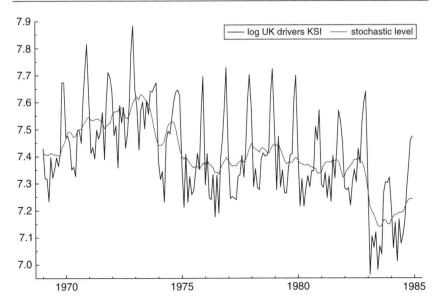

Figure 4.6. Stochastic level.

stochastic level and seasonal obtained from this analysis are displayed in Figures 4.6 and 4.7, respectively. The variance of the seasonal disturbances is very small. This indicates that the seasonal pattern in the observed time series hardly changes over the years, which is confirmed by inspection of Figure 4.7.

For a better understanding of the interpretation of the seasonal component in Figure 4.7, we focus on the first year of the seasonal component (i.e. on 1969), see Figure 4.8. It shows that the largest number of drivers in Great Britain were killed or seriously injured in the months of November and December of 1969, while April 1969 resulted in the smallest number. This pattern is repeated in all the other years of the series.

The irregular component for the stochastic level and seasonal model is displayed in Figure 4.9. The residuals of the stochastic model are much closer to independent random values than those obtained with the deterministic model (see Figure 4.5). Whether 'much closer' is close enough can be determined by the diagnostic tests in Table 4.2.

The first autocorrelation in the correlogram does not deviate from zero but also the autocorrelation at lag 12 is close to zero. This is the first of our analyses where we yield such a satisfactory result for this KSI series. In all previous analyses of the series, the autocorrelation at lag 12 was found to be unacceptably large, see Tables 2.1, 2.2, 3.1, and 3.2.

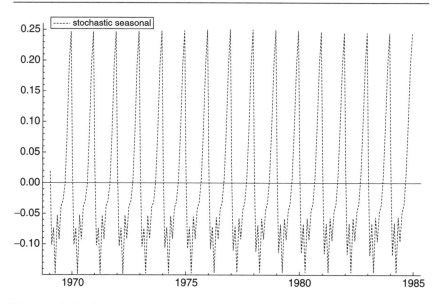

Figure 4.7. Stochastic seasonal.

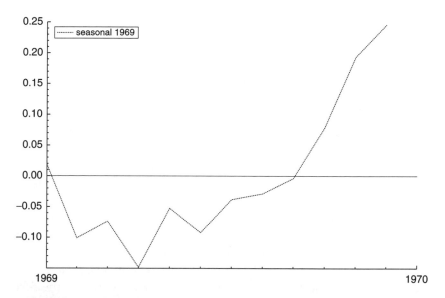

Figure 4.8. Stochastic seasonal for the year 1969.

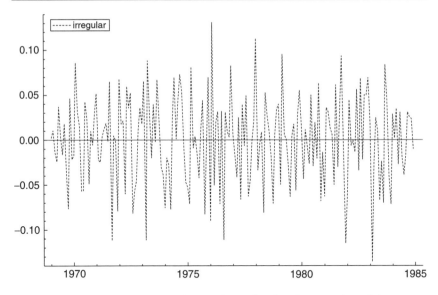

Figure 4.9. Irregular component for stochastic level and seasonal model.

The same applies to the general Q-test for independence based on the first 15 autocorrelations, which is for the first time smaller than the critical value of $\chi^2_{(13;0.05)} = 22.36$. The reason of these satisfactory results is that the the seasonality is explicitly modelled in the present analysis, whereas the residuals of the local level and local linear trend model contained the neglected seasonality in monthly data. Since the assumptions of homoscedasticity and normality are also realistic (see Table 4.2), the residuals of this analysis satisfy all the required criteria.

The Akaike information criterion for the stochastic level and seasonal model equals

$$\text{AIC} = \frac{1}{192}\left[-2(192)(0.9369063) + 2(12 + 3)\right] = -1.71756,$$

Table 4.2. Diagnostic tests for stochastic level and seasonal model and log UK drivers KSI.

	statistic	value	critical value	assumption satisfied
independence	$Q(15)$	14.150	22.36	+
	$r(1)$	0.039	±0.14	+
	$r(12)$	0.014	±0.14	+
homoscedasticity	$H(60)$	1.060	1.67	+
normality	N	5.289	5.99	+

41

indicating that this is the preferred model for the log of the UK drivers KSI series so far, even though it requires the estimation of a total of 15 parameters: one variance for the irregular component, two variances for the level and seasonal component, and 12 initial values of the state (one for the level, and 11 for the seasonal). Moreover, the present model also fits the data much better than the classical multiple regression analysis obtained with deterministic level and seasonal components.

Since the variance of the seasonal disturbances is found to be almost zero, in the next section we present the results of the analysis of the UK drivers KSI series with a stochastic level and a deterministic seasonal.

4.3. Stochastic level and deterministic seasonal

Fixing the seasonal disturbances ω_t in model (4.1) to zero, but still allowing the level to vary over time yields the following results:

```
it0    f=   0.9362753 df= 0.003305 e1=   0.01239 e2= 0.0001078
it1    f=   0.9362925 df= 0.003487 e1=   0.01310 e2= 0.0003366
it2    f=   0.9363240 df= 0.002234 e1=  0.008362 e2= 0.0003377
it3    f=   0.9363352 df= 0.001322 e1=  0.004066 e2= 0.0002726
it4    f=   0.9363361 df= 0.0002666 e1= 0.0008200 e2=4.323e-005
it5    f=   0.9363361 df=1.145e-005 e1=3.522e-005 e2=8.119e-006
Strong convergence
```

At convergence the value of the log-likelihood function is 0.9363361. The maximum likelihood estimate of the variance of the irregular component is $\widehat{\sigma}_\varepsilon^2 = 0.00351385$, and the maximum likelihood estimate of the variance of the level disturbances is $\widehat{\sigma}_\xi^2 = 0.000945723$. Plots of the results of this analysis are not shown here, because they are very similar to the ones presented in Section 4.2. The same applies to the results of the diagnostic tests which are very similar to those given in Table 4.2.

The Akaike information criterion for this model equals

$$\text{AIC} = \frac{1}{192}\left[-2(192)(0.9363361) + 2(12 + 2)\right] = -1.72684$$

indicating a slight improvement upon the previous model: the small reduction in the value of the log-likelihood function is compensated by the fact that the present model requires the estimation of only two variances instead of three in the previous model.

The AIC value of -1.72684 for the stochastic level and deterministic seasonal model is a significant improvement upon the local level model, which yields an AIC value of -1.25914. Therefore, and in contrast with the slope component, the addition of a seasonal component is essential in obtaining a good description of the time series at hand.

In this chapter the first *realistic and appropriate description* of the log of the number of UK drivers KSI is presented by combining a stochastic level with a deterministic seasonal component. Furthermore it is shown that a stochastic state space model can be reduced to its equivalent classical regression model by *fixing all state disturbances to zero*. This means that classical linear regression models can be viewed as deterministic state space models.

4.4. The local level and seasonal model and UK inflation

We end this chapter by discussing the results of the analysis of a time series consisting of quarterly UK inflation figures (as given in Appendix D, and displayed at the top of Figure 4.10) with the local level and seasonal model. In economics, the inflation is an important variable that refers to a rise in the general level of prices (deflation usually refers to a fall in prices). Economic policy makers find it important to have a good estimate of inflation. In practice, inflation is taken as the relative price change, usually expressed in a percentage.

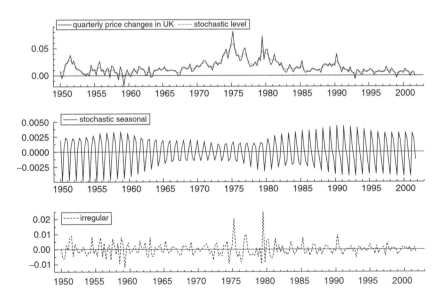

Figure 4.10. Stochastic level, seasonal and irregular in UK inflation series.

The percentage change of the price level over a quarter is not considered to be a reliable estimator of inflation. Instead, quarterly time series of price changes are analysed by time series models to assess inflation. The local level model is an appropriate candidate for this purpose. The final estimate of the level is then an appropriate estimator of the underlying rate of inflation as this represents the underlying inflation for the intermediate and longer term. Inflation relates to average household purchases that can be subject to seasonal variations due to events such as Christmas and summer holiday. As we are dealing with quarterly data, we include a stochastic seasonal component with a periodicity of $s = 4$ in the local level model. This approach of measuring inflation is illustrated by applying it to quarterly price changes in the United Kingdom for the 52 years from 1950 through to 2001 (yielding a total of $n = 52 \times 4 = 208$ observations). The estimation of the parameters in model (4.1) applied to the UK inflation series gives the following results:

```
it0    f=    3.023196 df=    0.1800 e1=    1.119 e2=  0.002894
it1    f=    3.069515 df=    0.1586 e1=    1.015 e2=  0.01299
it2    f=    3.164341 df=    0.1016 e1=    0.5279 e2=  0.01150
it5    f=    3.194490 df=    0.02758 e1=    0.1484 e2=  0.001452
it10   f=    3.198464 df=4.081e-005 e1= 0.0002241 e2=5.183e-005
it11   f=    3.198464 df=3.960e-006 e1=2.175e-005 e2=3.472e-006
Strong convergence
```

At convergence the value of the log-likelihood function is 3.198464. The maximum likelihood estimate of the irregular variance is $\hat{\sigma}_\varepsilon^2 = 3.3717 \times 10^{-5}$ and the maximum likelihood estimates of the variances of the level and seasonal disturbances are equal to $\hat{\sigma}_\xi^2 = 2.1197 \times 10^{-5}$ and $\hat{\sigma}_\omega^2 = 0.0109 \times 10^{-5}$, respectively.

The estimate of the final value of the level at time point $t = 208$ is $\hat{\mu}_{208} = 0.0020426$. This is our estimate of inflation. As a result, relative prices have increased overall by 0.20% in the final months of 2001. This is rather low. The evolution of inflation over time is reflected by the estimated level component and is presented in the upper graph of Figure 4.10, together with the observed price changes. It is noteworthy that the periods of highest inflation in the UK occurred in the middle of the 1970s and at the end of the 1970s. These periods coincide with the well-known oil and energy crises in the 1970s.

Graphs of the stochastic seasonal and irregular components are also displayed in Figure 4.10. Although the variance of the seasonal disturbances is smaller than that of the other two components, the changes over time in the estimated seasonal component of inflation series are clearly visible. The level component reflects the underlying level of inflation and

Table 4.3. Diagnostic tests for local level and seasonal model and UK inflation series.

	statistic	value	critical value	assumption satisfied
independence	Q(10)	7.573	15.507	+
	r(1)	0.049	±0.14	+
	r(4)	−0.0622	±0.14	+
homoscedasticity	H(68)	2.738	1.48	−
normality	N	171.550	5.99	−

its evolution over time is quite smooth. The residuals of this level plus seasonal model are close to independent random values (white noise). Some outlier observations appear in the irregular component but apart from these, the residuals seem quite random. Whether the residuals of the local level and seasonal model are close enough to a random process (see Section 10.1.2 for the definition of a random process) can be established by inspection of the diagnostic tests given in Table 4.3.

The last column in Table 4.3 shows that the diagnostics for independence are quite satisfactory. However, the assumptions of homoscedasticity and normality tests are clearly violated. The local level and seasonal model is therefore able to represent the dynamic features in the UK inflation series, but there are also some aspects in the series that still need to be accounted for. Specifically, the neglect in the present model of the large shocks in the estimated irregular component for the UK inflation series at the time points corresponding to the second quarter of 1975 and to the third quarter of 1979 deserve closer attention. It should not come as a surprise that these two time points are related to the world-wide oil and energy crises in the 1970s. An appropriate treatment of these 'outlier observations' will be discussed in Section 7.4.

The AIC for the present model equals

$$\text{AIC} = \frac{1}{208} [-2(208)(3.198464) + 2(4 + 3)] = -6.32962,$$

and this value will be used for reference purposes in Chapter 7.

In Chapters 5 and 6, components of the state are introduced that can be used to obtain *explanations* for the observed developments of a time series. The discussion of these components will be illustrated by adding them to the UK drivers KSI series. To keep the exposition as simple as possible, the seasonal component will temporarily be removed from these analyses, even though this component is clearly essential in describing the UK drivers KSI series. In the next two chapters, we are not concerned with the appropriateness of the models when applied to the UK drivers KSI series (and diagnostic residual tests will therefore not be presented). We mainly focus on various issues concerning the inclusion of explanatory variables in the state space models of Chapters 2 and 3. Nevertheless, in Chapter 7 – where a model is presented for the combined *description* and *explanation* of the log of the UK number of drivers KSI – the seasonal component will be added to the state equations.

5

The local level model with explanatory variable

To investigate the effects of other variables on the development of a particular time series, the explanatory or regression variables can be added to the measurement equation of the model. If regression variables are added to the local level model, for example, then the measurement equation becomes

$$y_t = \mu_t + \sum_{j=1}^{k} \beta_{jt} x_{jt} + \varepsilon_t, \tag{5.1}$$

where x_{jt} is a continuous predictor variable and β_{jt} is an unknown regression weight or coefficient, for $j = 1, \ldots, k$. For one predictor variable with $\beta_t = \beta_{1t}$, the model takes the form

$$
\begin{aligned}
y_t &= \mu_t + \beta_t x_t + \varepsilon_t, & \varepsilon_t &\sim \mathrm{NID}(0, \sigma_\varepsilon^2) \\
\mu_{t+1} &= \mu_t + \xi_t, & \xi_t &\sim \mathrm{NID}(0, \sigma_\xi^2) \\
\beta_{t+1} &= \beta_t + \tau_t, & \tau_t &\sim \mathrm{NID}(0, \sigma_\tau^2)
\end{aligned}
\tag{5.2}
$$

for $t = 1, \ldots, n$. The modelling of k explanatory variables requires k additional state equations, one for each explanatory variable. The state disturbances τ_t for the regression component in (5.2) are usually fixed on zero to establish a stable relationship between y_t and x_t for all t. As model (5.2) indicates, however, if required a stochastic regression component can be incorporated in the state space methodology. In the next two sections the results are presented of applying both the deterministic and the stochastic level model to the log of UK drivers KSI series, including one explanatory variable.

5.1. Deterministic level and explanatory variable

Fixing all state disturbances ξ_t and τ_t in (4.1) to zero, we have

for $t = 1$: $\qquad y_1 = \mu_1 + \beta_1 x_1 + \varepsilon_1,$

$\qquad\qquad\qquad \mu_2 = \mu_1 + \xi_1 = \mu_1 + 0 = \mu_1$

$\qquad\qquad\qquad \beta_2 = \beta_1 + \tau_1 = \beta_1 + 0 = \beta_1$

for $t = 2$: $\qquad y_2 = \mu_2 + \beta_2 x_2 + \varepsilon_2 = \mu_1 + \beta_1 x_2 + \varepsilon_2,$

$\qquad\qquad\qquad \mu_3 = \mu_2 + \xi_2 = \mu_2 + 0 = \mu_1$

$\qquad\qquad\qquad \beta_3 = \beta_2 + \tau_2 = \beta_2 + 0 = \beta_1$

for $t = 3$: $\qquad y_3 = \mu_3 + \beta_3 x_3 + \varepsilon_3 = \mu_1 + \beta_1 x_3 + \varepsilon_3,$

$\qquad\qquad\qquad \mu_4 = \mu_3 + \xi_3 = \mu_3 + 0 = \mu_1$

$\qquad\qquad\qquad \beta_4 = \beta_3 + \tau_3 = \beta_3 + 0 = \beta_1$

and so on.

Therefore, in this case the level model with explanatory variable simplifies to

$$y_t = \mu_1 + \beta_1 x_t + \varepsilon_t, \qquad \varepsilon_t \sim \mathrm{NID}(0, \sigma_\varepsilon^2) \qquad (5.3)$$

for $t = 1, \ldots, n$, where μ_1 and β_1 are the values of the level and the regression coefficient at the beginning of the series and apply to all t.

For example, taking the variable TIME $= 1, 2, \ldots, 192$ as the predictor variable, and fixing the state disturbances η_t and τ_t in (5.2) to zero, yields the following results:

```
it0    f=    0.4140728 df=1.287e-006 e1=3.715e-006 e2=4.460e-008
Strong convergence
```

Again the estimation of the parameters of this deterministic model requires no iterations. The value of the log-likelihood function is 0.4140728. The maximum likelihood estimate of the variance of the observation disturbances is 0.0229981, and the maximum likelihood estimates of μ_1 and β_1 are 7.5458 and -0.00145, respectively. Therefore, this state space model provides a classical linear regression analysis for the log of UK drivers KSI on time (see also Chapter 1 and Section 3.1). The regression equation is

$$\hat{y}_t = 7.5458 - 0.00145\, x_t$$

for $t = 1, \ldots, n$, with a residual variance of $\hat{\sigma}_\varepsilon^2 = 0.0229981$.

The plot of the combined deterministic level and regression components is identical to the regression line in Figure 1.1, and the residuals of the deterministic level model with explanatory variable TIME are identical to the residuals shown in Figure 1.3.

The value of the Akaike information criterion for this model equals

$$\text{AIC} = \frac{1}{192}\,[-2(192)(0.4140728) + 2(2 + 1)] = -0.796896,$$

which is identical to the AIC value obtained with the deterministic linear trend model (see Section 3.1), as expected.

More generally, and in contrast with the deterministic linear trend model, the present state space model allows a classical regression analysis using *any* continuous predictor variable. For example, in the period 1969–1984 the price of petrol in the UK showed substantial variations (see Appendix A). Higher petrol prices may well have resulted in a reduction of the number of vehicles circulating in traffic, thus reducing the number of drivers killed or seriously injured. Such a hypothesis can be investigated by inserting the log of the monthly petrol prices in the UK as an explanatory variable in model (5.3). This yields the following results:

```
it0     f=      0.4457201 df=7.918e-007 e1=2.285e-006 e2=2.744e-008
Strong convergence
```

The optimum of the log-likelihood function equals 0.4457201. The maximum likelihood estimate of the variance of the irregular disturbances is 0.0230137, and the maximum likelihood estimates of μ_1 and β_1 are $\widehat{\mu}_1 = 5.8787$ and $\widehat{\beta}_1 = -0.67166$, respectively. This state space model yields a classical linear regression solution, with regression equation

$$\hat{y}_t = 5.8787 - 0.67166\,x_t \tag{5.4}$$

for $t = 1, \ldots, n$, and error variance $\widehat{\sigma}_\varepsilon^2 = 0.0230137$. The negative value of $\widehat{\beta}_1$ indicates a negative relationship between the number of drivers KSI and petrol price: lower petrol prices are associated with more drivers killed and seriously injured, and vice versa. Moreover, since the predictor and criterion variable are in logarithms, the regression coefficient β_1 may be interpreted as what is known as an *elasticity*, a well-known concept in the economic literature (see, e.g., Varian, 1999).

Generally, elasticity is defined as the *percent* change in y divided by the *percent* change in x, and can be written algebraically as

$$s^* = \frac{x}{y}\,\frac{\partial y}{\partial x}. \tag{5.5}$$

Since the predictor and criterion variables in (5.3) are in logarithms, the regression equation actually equals

$$\log y = a + b \log x, \tag{5.6}$$

where y here denotes the actual monthly numbers of drivers killed or seriously injured, and x the actual monthly petrol prices. The subscripts t have temporarily been omitted in (5.6) to simplify notation. Taking the exponent of (5.6) to re-express the relation in terms of the original variables y and x yields

$$e^{\log y} = e^{a+b \log x},$$

and therefore

$$y = e^a\, e^{b \log x} = e^a\, x^b = c\, x^b, \tag{5.7}$$

with $c = e^a$. Applying (5.5) to (5.7), the elasticity value equals

$$s^* = \frac{x}{c\,x^b}\, \frac{\partial c\,x^b}{\partial x} = \frac{x}{c\,x^b}\, \frac{c\,b\,x^b}{x} = b. \tag{5.8}$$

This shows that the curve defined by $y = c\,x^b$ satisfies the special property of *constant elasticity*. In the present case, the value of $\hat{\beta}_1 = -0.67$ in (5.4) therefore indicates that a 1% increase in the petrol price resulted in a 0.67% decrease in the numbers of drivers KSI.

Figure 5.1 shows the development of the estimated level and explanatory variable 'log petrol price' as a function of time. In Figure 5.2 the results of the same analysis are shown as is usual in a classical regression context: displaying the regression line in the scatter plot of dependent variable y_t against the predictor variable 'log petrol price'. The residuals for this analysis are displayed in Figure 5.3.

The Akaike information criterion for this deterministic model equals

$$\text{AIC} = \frac{1}{192}\,[-2(192)(0.4457201) + 2(2+1)] = -0.86019.$$

Since the model requires the maximum likelihood estimation of two initial elements, and one variance (of the irregular component), we have the term $(2+1)$ in the calculation of the AIC.

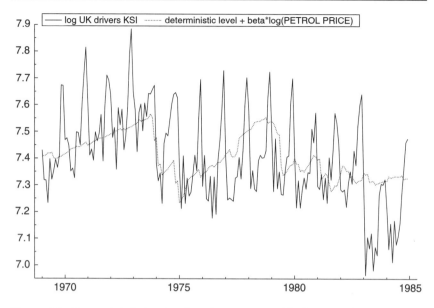

Figure 5.1. Deterministic level and explanatory variable 'log petrol price'.

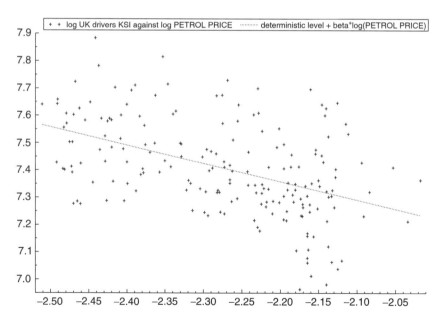

Figure 5.2. Conventional classical regression representation of deterministic level and explanatory variable 'log petrol price'.

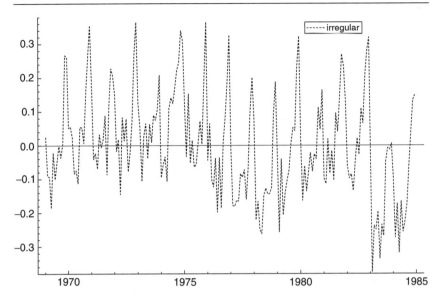

Figure 5.3. Irregular component for deterministic level model with explanatory variable 'log petrol price'.

5.2. Stochastic level and explanatory variable

The analysis of the local level model with explanatory variable 'log petrol price' and for which the level in model (5.2) is allowed to vary over time, yields the following results.

```
it0    f=    0.5733865 df=    0.07555 e1=    0.2408 e2=  0.003029
it1    f=    0.5845338 df=    0.09740 e1=    0.3031 e2=   0.2138
it2    f=    0.6351207 df=    0.06160 e1=    0.1661 e2=   0.01541
it3    f=    0.6426605 df=    0.03384 e1=    0.1028 e2=  0.005960
it4    f=    0.6433967 df=    0.03190 e1=  0.09833 e2=  0.001475
it5    f=    0.6443015 df=    0.03043 e1=  0.07582 e2=  0.001665
it6    f=    0.6454830 df=    0.01032 e1=  0.02562 e2=  0.002765
it7    f=    0.6456257 df=  0.001269 e1=  0.004136 e2=  0.001098
it8    f=    0.6456353 df= 0.0005193 e1=  0.001287 e2= 0.0003957
it9    f=    0.6456361 df= 0.0001071 e1= 0.0002651 e2= 0.0001274
it10   f=    0.6456361 df=9.594e-006 e1=2.375e-005 e2=8.169e-006
Strong convergence
```

At convergence the value of the log-likelihood function is 0.6456361. The maximum likelihood estimate of the variance of the observation disturbances is 0.00234791, and that of the variance of the level disturbances equals 0.0116673. The maximum likelihood estimates of μ_1 and β_1 are $\widehat{\mu_1} = 6.8204$ and $\widehat{\beta_1} = -0.26105$, respectively. The negative value of β_1 again indicates a negative relationship between the number of drivers KSI and petrol price. Interpreting β_1 as an elasticity (see Section 5.1), the

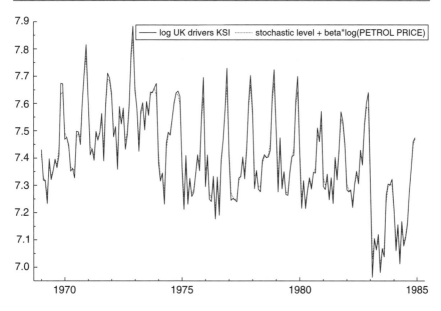

Figure 5.4. Stochastic level and deterministic explanatory variable 'log petrol price'.

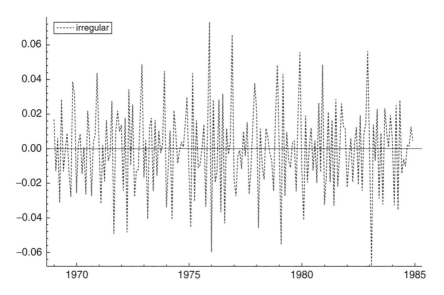

Figure 5.5. Irregular for stochastic level model with deterministic explanatory variable 'log petrol price'.

present model suggests that a 1% increase in petrol price was associated with a 0.26% decrease in the number of drivers KSI on UK roads.

Figure 5.4 contains the graph of the stochastic level and deterministic explanatory variable 'log petrol price', while Figure 5.5 shows the irregular component corresponding to this model. The differences between these disturbances and the ones displayed in Figure 5.3 are noticeable.

The Akaike information criterion for this model equals

$$AIC = \frac{1}{192}[-2(192)(0.6456361) + 2(2+2)] = -1.24961,$$

indicating an important improvement upon the classical regression model with deterministic level and explanatory variable 'log of petrol price'.

For the moment, we do not draw any practical conclusions from the analyses of the UK drivers KSI series presented in this chapter as an essential component is missing in model (5.2), which is the seasonal.

6

The local level model with intervention variable

In time series analysis of road traffic safety data, for example, it is often required to be able to assess the effect of road safety measures on the development in traffic safety over time. In state space methods such effects can be evaluated by adding *intervention variables* to any of the models discussed in the previous chapters.

There are a number of different ways in which interventions can be expected to influence the development in a time series. One possible effect is that of a *level shift*, where the value of the level of the time series suddenly changes at the time point where the intervention took place, and where the level change is permanent after the intervention. A second possible effect is that of a *slope shift* in the series. In this case it is the value of the slope that shows a significant and permanent change after the intervention was made. A third possible effect is that of a *pulse*, where the value of the level suddenly changes at the moment of the intervention, and then immediately returns to the value before the intervention took place. The latter effect only affects the current observation and is temporary.

Below we will present a detailed assessment of the level shift. In February 1983, the seat belt law was introduced in the UK. To investigate whether the introduction of this law resulted in a level shift in the log of the monthly number of drivers KSI in the UK, an intervention variable is added to the local level model, as follows:

$$y_t = \mu_t + \lambda_t\, w_t + \varepsilon_t, \quad \varepsilon_t \sim \mathrm{NID}(0, \sigma_\varepsilon^2)$$

$$\mu_{t+1} = \mu_t + \xi_t, \qquad\qquad \xi_t \sim \mathrm{NID}(0, \sigma_\xi^2) \qquad\qquad (6.1)$$

$$\lambda_{t+1} = \lambda_t + \rho_t, \qquad\qquad \rho_t \sim \mathrm{NID}(0, \sigma_\rho^2)$$

for $t = 1, \ldots, n$. In (6.1), the dummy variable w_t equals zero at all time points before the introduction of the seat belt law, and equals unity at time points after the introduction of the law. The coefficient $\lambda_1 = \lambda_t$ is treated as a fixed regression parameter. Therefore, the state disturbances ρ_t in (6.1) are fixed to zero for all $t = 1, \ldots, n$. In this way, an intervention effect is introduced in the model. Since the seat belt law was introduced in February 1983, the first 169 values of w_t are set to zero, whereas the last 23 values are set to unity.

In the next two sections, the results are discussed of adding this intervention variable to both a deterministic and a stochastic level model.

6.1. Deterministic level and intervention variable

Analogous to Section 5.1 where both the level and the intervention variable are treated deterministically, model (6.1) simplifies to

$$y_t = \mu_1 + \lambda_1 w_t + \varepsilon_t, \qquad \varepsilon_t \sim \text{NID}(0, \sigma_\varepsilon^2) \qquad (6.2)$$

for $t = 1, \ldots, n$, where μ_1 and λ_1 are the values of μ_t and λ_t for all time periods $t = 1, \ldots, n$.

When the seat belt intervention variable w_t is added to the level model, and the state disturbances ξ_t and ρ_t in (6.1) are fixed to zero, the following results are obtained:

```
it0    f=     0.4573681 df=1.297e-006 e1=3.764e-006 e2=4.466e-008
Strong convergence
```

Since the model is completely deterministic, no iterations are required. The value of the log-likelihood function is 0.4573681. The maximum likelihood estimate of the variance of the irregular component is 0.0222426, and the maximum likelihood estimates of μ_1 and λ_1 are $\widehat{\mu}_1 = 7.4374$ and $\widehat{\lambda}_1 = -0.26111$, respectively.

Therefore, this state space model yields a classical linear regression solution with regression equation

$$\hat{y}_t = 7.4374 - 0.26111 \, w_t \qquad (6.3)$$

and residual variance $\widehat{\sigma}_\varepsilon^2 = 0.0222426$.

In Figure 6.1 the combined deterministic level and intervention variable are plotted against time. The figure clearly illustrates why this type of intervention effect is called a *level shift*: from February 1983 onwards there is a sudden drop of 0.26111 units in the level of the series.

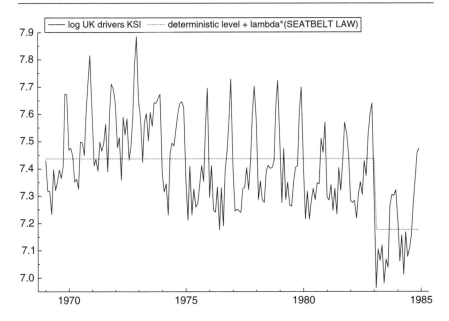

Figure 6.1. Deterministic level and intervention variable.

In Figure 6.2 the results of the same analysis are shown as is usual in a classical regression context: by drawing the regression line in the scatter plot of dependent variable y_t against the dummy predictor variable w_t.

The regression line in Figure 6.2 is the line connecting the two points with coordinates $(0, 7.4372)$ and $(1, 7.1756)$, respectively. Letting $\bar{y}_1$ denote the mean of the log of the number of UK drivers KSI in the first 169 time points of the series, and $\bar{y}_2$ the mean of the log of the number of UK drivers KSI in the last 23 time points of the series, it is interesting to note that $\bar{y}_1 = 7.4374$ and $\bar{y}_2 = 7.1763$. Therefore, equation (6.3) can be written as

$$\hat{y}_t = \bar{y}_1 + (\bar{y}_2 - \bar{y}_1)\, w_t \qquad (6.4)$$

for $t = 1, \ldots, n$, and the present analysis is actually a one-way ANOVA with two treatment levels (see, e.g., Kirk, 1968). The t-ratio for the regression weight in (6.3) equals $t = -7.877$, while the F-test for the ANOVA is $F = t^2 = (-7.877)^2 = 62.054$. Of course, both significance tests are seriously flawed because they are based on the assumption of random errors.

Since the intervention variable w_t is not in logarithms, the value of regression weight λ_1 cannot be interpreted as an elasticity, as was done in Chapter 5. Still, the percent change in the number of UK drivers KSI

The local level model with intervention variable

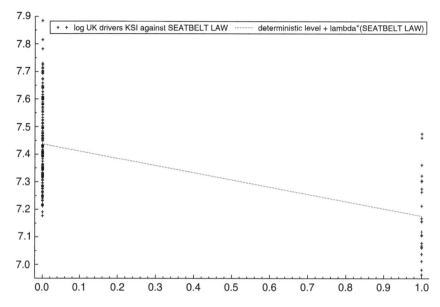

Figure 6.2. Conventional classical regression representation of deterministic level and intervention variable.

as a result of the intervention variable can be established as follows. Let $\hat{y}_{\text{pre}}$ denote the value of $\mu_1 + \lambda_1 w_t = \mu_1$ before the intervention, and $\hat{y}_{\text{post}}$ the value of $\mu_1 + \lambda_1 w_t = \mu_1 + \lambda_1$ after the intervention. Then – since y_t is in logarithms – the percent change due to the intervention equals

$$100 \left(\frac{e^{\hat{y}_{\text{post}}} - e^{\hat{y}_{\text{pre}}}}{e^{\hat{y}_{\text{pre}}}} \right),$$

where $e^{\hat{y}_{\text{pre}}} = e^{\mu_1 + \lambda_1 w_t} = e^{\mu_1}$ (since w_t is coded 0 before the intervention), and $e^{\hat{y}_{\text{post}}} = e^{\mu_1 + \lambda_1 w_{\text{post}}} = e^{\mu_1 + \lambda_1}$ (since w_t is coded 1 at and after the intervention), respectively. The percent change due to the seat belt law therefore equals

$$100 \left(\frac{e^{\mu_1 + \lambda_1} - e^{\mu_1}}{e^{\mu_1}} \right) = 100 \left(\frac{(e^{\mu_1})(e^{\lambda_1}) - e^{\mu_1}}{e^{\mu_1}} \right) = 100(e^{\lambda_1} - 1). \quad (6.5)$$

Since the deterministic level and intervention variable model leads to the estimate $\widehat{\lambda}_1 = -0.26111$, we conclude that the introduction of the seat belt law in the UK resulted in a reduction of 23% in the number of drivers killed or seriously injured. This follows from the calculation $100(e^{-0.26111} - 1) = -22.98$.

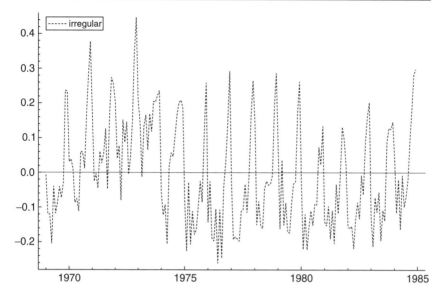

Figure 6.3. Irregular component for deterministic level model with intervention variable.

The residuals of this classical regression analysis are shown in Figure 6.3 and they display a very systematic pattern. It is interesting to note, however, that the large residual in February 1983 (in absolute terms) observed in the irregular component of all previous deterministic analyses (see Figures 2.2, 4.5, and 5.3) is no longer present in Figure 6.3.

The Akaike information criterion for the deterministic level and intervention variable model equals

$$\text{AIC} = \frac{1}{192}\left[-2(192)(0.4573681) + 2(2+1)\right] = -0.883486,$$

showing that for the log of the UK drivers KSI this is the best fitting deterministic model so far.

6.2. Stochastic level and intervention variable

The analysis where the level of model (6.1) is allowed to vary over time yields the following results:

```
it0    f=    0.6002860 df=  0.07065 e1=   0.2274 e2=  0.002798
it1    f=    0.6099381 df=  0.09065 e1=   0.2854 e2=   0.1146
it2    f=    0.6573212 df=  0.04074 e1=   0.1099 e2=  0.01672
it3    f=    0.6610085 df=  0.02811 e1=  0.08506 e2=  0.003747
```

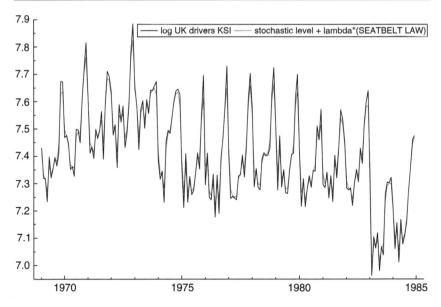

Figure 6.4. Stochastic level and intervention variable.

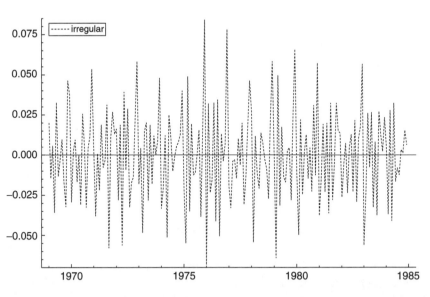

Figure 6.5. Irregular component for stochastic level model with intervention variable.

```
it4     f=      0.6617649 df=    0.02642 e1=    0.08131 e2=  0.001678
it5     f=      0.6623236 df=    0.02294 e1=    0.06187 e2=  0.001210
it6     f=      0.6630441 df=   0.004739 e1=    0.01336 e2=  0.002168
it7     f=      0.6630834 df= 0.0005152 e1=   0.001650 e2= 0.0005872
it8     f=      0.6630850 df= 0.0001960 e1= 0.0004964 e2= 0.0001568
it9     f=      0.6630851 df=2.574e-005 e1=6.519e-005 e2=2.906e-005
Strong convergence
```

At convergence the value of the log-likelihood function is 0.6630851. The maximum likelihood estimate of the irregular variance is 0.00269276, and that of the variance of the level disturbances equals 0.0104111. The maximum likelihood estimates of μ_1 and λ_1 are $\widehat{\mu}_1 = 7.4107$ and $\widehat{\lambda}_1 = -0.3785$. Since $e^{-0.3785} - 1 = -0.315$ (see Section 6.1), according to this model the introduction of the seat belt law in the UK resulted in a 31.5% reduction of the absolute numbers of drivers KSI.

The sum of the stochastic level and deterministic intervention components is presented in Figure 6.4. The irregular component of the present model is shown in Figure 6.5. Again, the difference in randomness between Figures 6.3 and 6.5 is very noticeable. Also, the large negative residual observed for the month of February 1983 in the plots of the irregular component of all previous stochastic analyses of the UK data (see Figures 2.4, 3.3, 4.9, and 5.5) has disappeared in Figure 6.5. This is the result of including the intervention variable in the state space model.

The Akaike information criterion for this model equals

$$\text{AIC} = \frac{1}{192}\left[-2(192)(0.6630851) + 2(2+2)\right] = -1.2845,$$

which is again better than the deterministic level and intervention model. Again, we do not draw any practical conclusions from these two intervention analyses until the seasonal has been reintroduced into the model. This is done in the following chapter.

7

The UK seat belt and inflation models

Combining all the state components discussed in the previous chapters, we obtain the first realistic model for both *describing* and *explaining* the development of the monthly number of drivers KSI in UK road accidents in the period 1969–1984. Level, seasonal, the log of petrol price and the introduction of the seat belt law in February 1983 are combined into the following model:

$$y_t = \mu_t + \gamma_{1,t} + \beta_t \, x_t + \lambda_t \, w_t + \varepsilon_t, \quad \varepsilon_t \sim \text{NID}(0, \sigma_\varepsilon^2)$$

$$\mu_{t+1} = \mu_t + \xi_t, \quad \xi_t \sim \text{NID}(0, \sigma_\xi^2)$$

$$\gamma_{1,t+1} = -\gamma_{1,t} - \gamma_{2,t} - \gamma_{3,t} + \omega_t, \quad \omega_t \sim \text{NID}(0, \sigma_\omega^2)$$

$$\gamma_{2,t+1} = \gamma_{1,t}, \tag{7.1}$$

$$\gamma_{3,t+1} = \gamma_{2,t},$$

$$\beta_{t+1} = \beta_t + \tau_t, \quad \tau_t \sim \text{NID}(0, \sigma_\tau^2)$$

$$\lambda_{t+1} = \lambda_t + \rho_t, \quad \rho_t \sim \text{NID}(0, \sigma_\rho^2)$$

for $t = 1, \ldots, n$, where x_t is the continuous predictor variable 'log petrol price', and w_t is the dummy variable consisting of zeroes at all time points before the introduction of the seat belt law in February 1983, and ones at time points of and after the introduction in February 1983. It is important to note that model (7.1) is presented for quarterly data. The actual model requires a total of 14 state equations since the UK drivers KSI series consists of monthly observations. Results of the analysis of the UK drivers KSI series with deterministic and stochastic components are presented in Sections 7.1 through 7.3. In Section 7.4 model (7.1) is also applied to the quarterly UK inflation series previously presented in Section 4.4. In that case, however, the variables x_t and w_t consist of pulse intervention variables.

7.1. Deterministic level and seasonal

Fixing all state disturbances ξ_t, ω_t, τ_t, and ρ_t to zero for all t in model (7.1), we obtain the following estimation results:

```
it0    f=    0.8023778 df=2.913e-006 e1=1.006e-005 e2=8.437e-008
Strong convergence
```

Since the model is completely deterministic, no iterations during the estimation process are required. The value of the log-likelihood function is 0.8023778, and the maximum likelihood estimate of the variance of the observation disturbances is $\widehat{\sigma}_\varepsilon^2 = 0.00740223$. The maximum likelihood estimate of the level at the beginning of the series is $\widehat{\mu}_1 = 6.4016$. The maximum likelihood estimates of the regression weights for the log of petrol price and for the intervention variable at the beginning of the series are $\widehat{\beta}_1 = -0.45213$ and $\widehat{\lambda}_1 = -0.19714$, respectively. Interpreting β_1 as an elasticity, and keeping all other components constant, an increase of 1% in petrol price is associated with a 0.45% decrease in the number of drivers killed or seriously injured. Moreover, since $e^{-0.19714} - 1 = -0.179$, this model suggests a reduction of 17.9% in the actual numbers of drivers KSI as a result of the introduction of the seat belt law.

It may be noted that a classical multiple regression analysis with the dummy coding scheme for the seasonal effect described in Section 4.1, together with the log of petrol price and an additional dummy variable for the intervention in February 1983, yields identical results. The combined deterministic level and effects of the explanatory and intervention variables are displayed in Figure 7.1. Inspection of the diagnostic tests in Table 7.1 shows that the assumptions of homoscedasticity and normality are met in this analysis, but not the most important assumption of residual independence.

The Akaike information criterion for this analysis equals

$$\text{AIC} = \frac{1}{192}\left[-2(192)(0.8023778) + 2(14 + 1)\right] = -1.44851,$$

meaning that, for the UK drivers KSI series, this is the best fitting deterministic (and therefore classical regression) model that we have presented so far.

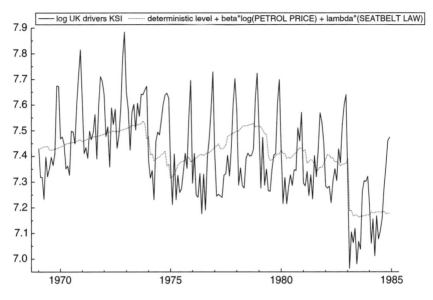

Figure 7.1. Deterministic level plus variables log petrol price and seat belt law.

7.2. Stochastic level and seasonal

When the level and the seasonal components in model (7.1) are allowed to vary over time, the estimation procedure yields the following results:

```
it0    f=    0.8182950 df=    0.08087 e1=    0.3864 e2= 0.001692
it5    f=    0.8955023 df=     0.1184 e1=    0.6119 e2=  0.01222
it10   f=    0.9792069 df=    0.01363 e1=   0.08855 e2= 0.007211
it15   f=    0.9822971 df=   0.003844 e1=   0.01596 e2= 0.0006901
it20   f=    0.9825225 df=5.511e-006 e1=2.328e-005 e2=7.949e-005
Strong convergence
```

At convergence the value of the log-likelihood function is 0.9825225, and the maximum likelihood estimate of the variance of the irregular is

Table 7.1. Diagnostic tests for the deterministic model applied to the UK drivers KSI series.

	statistic	value	critical value	assumption satisfied
independence	$Q(15)$	147.020	25.00	−
	$r(1)$	0.426	±0.14	−
	$r(12)$	0.198	±0.14	−
homoscedasticity	$1/H(59)$	1.110	1.67	+
normality	N	0.560	5.99	+

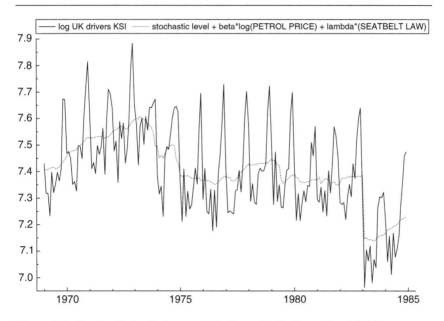

Figure 7.2. Stochastic level plus variables log petrol price and seat belt law.

$\widehat{\sigma}_\varepsilon^2$ = 0.00378629. The maximum likelihood estimates of the variances of the state disturbances are $\widehat{\sigma}_\xi^2$ = 0.000267632 and $\widehat{\sigma}_\omega^2$ = 0.0000011622. The maximum likelihood estimates of the regression weights for the log of petrol price and for the intervention variable at the beginning of the series are $\widehat{\beta}_1$ = −0.29141 and $\widehat{\lambda}_1$ = −0.23774, respectively. Keeping the other components constant and according to this model, a 1% increase in petrol price yields a 0.29% decrease in the number of drivers KSI. Moreover, since $e^{-0.23774} - 1 = -0.212$, this model indicates that the introduction of the seat belt law resulted in a reduction of 21.2% in the absolute numbers of drivers KSI.

The combined stochastic level and deterministic effects of the explanatory and intervention variables are displayed in Figure 7.2, while Figure 7.3 contains the stochastic seasonal. The irregular component for model (7.1) with stochastic level and seasonal is plotted in Figure 7.4.

As Table 7.2 shows, the residuals of this analysis do not indicate any departure from independence, homoscedasticity, and normality, and are therefore completely satisfactory. The Akaike information criterion for model (7.1) with stochastic level and seasonal equals

$$\text{AIC} = \frac{1}{192}\left[-2(192)(0.9825225) + 2(14 + 3)\right] = -1.78796.$$

65

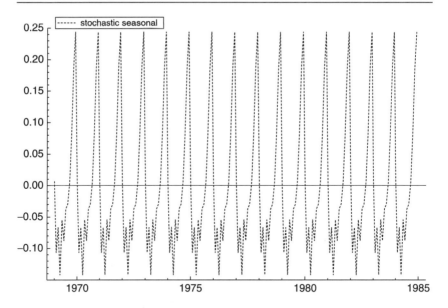

Figure 7.3. Stochastic seasonal.

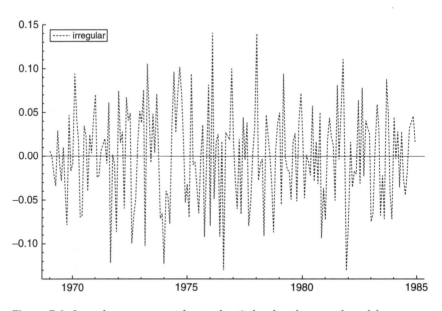

Figure 7.4. Irregular component for stochastic level and seasonal model.

Table 7.2. Diagnostic tests for the stochastic model applied to the UK drivers KSI series.

	statistic	value	critical value	assumption satisfied
independence	Q(15)	15.937	22.36	+
	r(1)	0.069	±0.14	+
	r(12)	0.025	±0.14	+
homoscedasticity	1/H(59)	1.110	1.67	+
normality	N	1.475	5.99	+

This is the best AIC so far. Since the variance for the stochastic seasonal is almost zero, in the next section we conclude the analysis by presenting the results of the analysis of model (7.1) with a stochastic level and a deterministic seasonal.

7.3. Stochastic level and deterministic seasonal

Modelling a stochastic level but a deterministic seasonal yields the following results:

```
it0    f=    0.9699348 df=    0.03177 e1=    0.1209 e2=  0.001020
it1    f=    0.9715092 df=    0.03493 e1=    0.1341 e2=  0.003300
it2    f=    0.9748103 df=    0.03373 e1=    0.1182 e2=  0.003195
it3    f=    0.9780184 df=    0.04283 e1=    0.1285 e2=  0.004638
it4    f=    0.9796652 df=    0.01785 e1=   0.05356 e2=  0.003426
it5    f=    0.9798642 df= 0.0005501 e1=  0.001654 e2=  0.001182
it6    f=    0.9798650 df=5.342e-005 e1= 0.0001606 e2= 0.0001097
it7    f=    0.9798650 df=6.202e-006 e1=1.865e-005 e2=8.033e-006
Strong convergence
```

At convergence the value of the log-likelihood function is 0.9798650, and the maximum likelihood estimate of the variance of the irregular component is $\widehat{\sigma}_\varepsilon^2 = 0.00403394$. The maximum likelihood estimate of the variance of the level disturbances is $\widehat{\sigma}_\xi^2 = 0.000268082$. The maximum likelihood estimates of the regression weights for the log of petrol price and for the intervention variable are $\widehat{\beta}_1 = -0.27674$ and $\widehat{\lambda}_1 = -0.23759$, respectively. In this case, a 1% increase in petrol price yields a 0.28% decrease in number of drivers KSI. The estimated reduction in the actual number of drivers KSI as a result of the introduction of the seat belt law is the same as in the previous model: 21.1% (note that $e^{-0.23759} - 1 = -0.211$).

Plots of the results of this analysis are not shown here, because they are virtually identical to the ones presented in Section 7.2. The diagnostic tests for the residuals are also very similar to those given in Table 7.2.

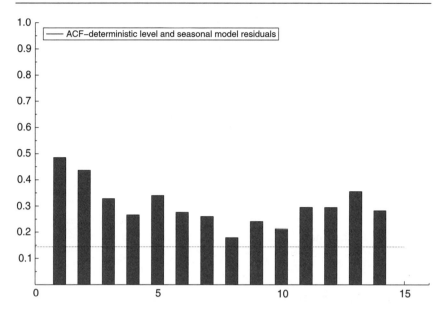

Figure 7.5. Correlogram of irregular component of completely deterministic level and seasonal model.

The Akaike information criterion for this model equals

$$AIC = \frac{1}{192}\left[-2(192)(0.9798650) + 2(14 + 2)\right] = -1.79306,$$

yielding a slightly better fit than the model with stochastic level and seasonal.

When the level component in (7.1) is allowed to vary over time and the seasonal effect is treated as a deterministic component, we obtain a model that can effectively be used for the analysis of the UK drivers KSI series. The model requires the estimation of 14 initial values of state variables and two variances. In contrast with the classical regression model discussed in Section 7.1, the residuals of the model with a stochastic level satisfy a selection of diagnostic statistics. Finally, to show the differences clearly, correlograms of the residuals of these analyses are presented in Figures 7.5 and 7.6. Twelve of the first 14 autocorrelations of the model with a stochastic level are within the 95% confidence limits of $\pm 2/\sqrt{n} = \pm 2/\sqrt{192} = \pm 0.144$ while those for a fully deterministic model are all outside this range. The latter case has serious implications for the significance tests of the regression coefficients for the explanatory and intervention variables, see the discussion in Chapter 1.

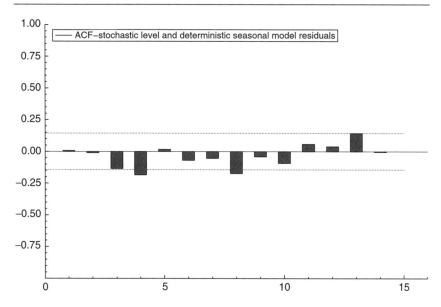

Figure 7.6. Correlogram of irregular component of stochastic level and deterministic seasonal model.

In the deterministic model corresponding to Figure 7.5, the estimated standard errors of the regression estimates, −0.45213 for the log of petrol price and −0.19714 for the intervention variable, are 0.05640 and 0.02073, respectively. Therefore, the *t*-ratio for the log of petrol price equals −0.45213/0.05640 = −8.01705, while the *t*-ratio for the intervention variable equals −0.19714/0.02073 = −9.51098. On the other hand, in the model with stochastic level and deterministic seasonal the estimated standard errors of the regression coefficients −0.27674 for the log of the petrol price and −0.23759 for the intervention variable are 0.098407 and 0.04645, respectively. Thus, the *t*-ratio for the log of the petrol price equals −0.27674/0.098407 = −2.81221 in this case, while the *t*-ratio for the intervention variable equals −0.23759/0.04645 = −5.11535. When the model with a stochastic level is taken as the true model, the *t*-ratio for the log of the petrol price in classical regression is over-estimated by 287%, while the *t*-ratio for the intervention variable is overestimated by 183%. In the present case all *t*-values happen to be significant at the 1% level, but it is not very difficult to see that classical regression may easily result in overoptimistic or even incorrect conclusions.

7.4. The UK inflation model

The analysis of the UK inflation time series discussed previously in Section 4.4 concerns the inflation in the UK, as measured on a quarterly basis for the years of 1950–2001 (see Appendix D). As mentioned in Section 4.4, the local level and seasonal model does provide an appropriate description of this time series. However, the diagnostics have not been fully satisfactory, and the model has not accounted for two inflation shocks that coincide with the oil and energy crises in the 1970s.

The inclusion of two intervention variables for the second quarter of 1975 and for the third quarter of 1979 is therefore considered in the analysis in this section. To this end, the local level and seasonal model discussed in Section 4.4 is extended by adding two *pulse intervention* variables to the model. A pulse intervention variable contains a one at the time point corresponding to the outlier observation, and zeroes elsewhere. Estimation of the parameters in model (7.1) (where x_t and w_t are pulse intervention variables) for the UK inflation series extending from 1950 to 2001 on a quarterly basis yields the following results:

```
it0    f=    3.124249 df=    0.1826 e1=    1.160 e2= 0.002872
it1    f=    3.172349 df=    0.1622 e1=    1.060 e2=  0.01354
it2    f=    3.272544 df=    0.1170 e1=   0.6254 e2=  0.01192
it5    f=    3.303308 df=   0.01574 e1=  0.08757 e2= 0.0009218
it10   f=    3.305023 df=2.155e-005 e1= 0.0001311 e2=4.425e-005
it11   f=    3.305023 df=4.115e-006 e1=2.287e-005 e2=3.060e-006
Strong convergence
```

At convergence the value of the log-likelihood function is 3.305023 which is higher than the likelihood reported in Section 4.4. The maximum likelihood estimate of the irregular variance is $\widehat{\sigma}_\varepsilon^2 = 2.1990 \times 10^{-5}$ and the maximum likelihood estimates of the state variances are given by $\widehat{\sigma}_\xi^2 = 1.8595 \times 10^{-5}$ and $\widehat{\sigma}_\omega^2 = 0.0110 \times 10^{-5}$. The estimates of the irregular and level variances in the model without the interventions in Section 4.4 are equal to 2.1198×10^{-5} and 0.0109×10^{-5}, respectively. The seasonal variance has not changed while the variance of the level disturbance has decreased somewhat due to the inclusion of the two pulse intervention variables.

However, the largest impact of the interventions is on the estimated variance of the irregular component. Its estimate in Section 4.4 was 3.3717×10^{-5}, which is larger than the one obtained in the current analysis, being 2.1990×10^{-5}. It is clear that the two pulse intervention variables have accounted for the two large residuals corresponding to the

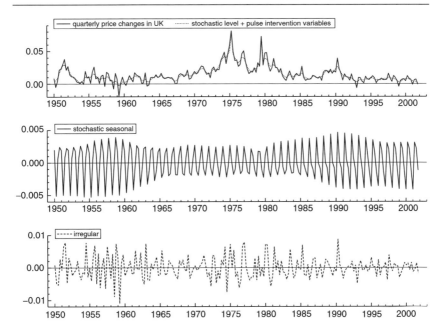

Figure 7.7. Local level (including pulse interventions), local seasonal and irregular for UK inflation time series data.

second quarter of 1975 and the third quarter of 1979 in the estimated irregular component in Section 4.4.

The stochastic level plus pulse intervention variables are displayed at the top of Figure 7.7, while the seasonal and irregular components are displayed in the middle and at the bottom of Figure 7.7. The estimated level and seasonal components are similar to those obtained in the earlier analysis discussed in Section 4.4. However, the stochastic level plus pulse intervention variables now capture the two large outlier observations in the second quarter of 1975 and in the third quarter of 1979 (see the top graph in Figure 7.7). The estimated irregular is also quite distinct from that obtained in the analysis of Section 4.4: the two outlier values in the second quarter of 1975 and in the third quarter of 1979 in Figure 4.10 have disappeared in the bottom graph of Figure 7.7.

The diagnostics presented in Table 7.3 have improved in comparison with those presented in Section 4.4. There is one notable difference. The normality test of the residuals of the model including the two pulse interventions is satisfactory, while the residuals for the model without interventions do not satisfy the assumption of normality at all (see Table 4.3).

Table 7.3. Diagnostic tests for the local level and seasonal model including pulse intervention variables for the UK inflation series.

	statistic	value	critical value	assumption satisfied
independence	$Q(10)$	11.644	12.59	+
	$r(1)$	0.0349	±0.14	+
	$r(4)$	−0.0703	±0.14	+
homoscedasticity	$H(67)$	2.504	1.48	−
normality	N	0.095	5.99	+

This may not be surprising since the two interventions remove the two large shocks in the residuals, resulting in a distribution of the residuals with tails that are not so heavy (compared to those with shocks). The remaining unsatisfactory diagnostic is that for homoscedasticity. Inspection of the estimated irregular in Figure 7.7 reveals that the variation at the beginning of the sample is indeed larger than at the end of the sample. This is clearly indicative of heteroscedasticity. This phenomenon in inflation series (and other macroeconomic time series) is recognised by many economists and is debated in the literature, see for example Stock and Watson (1996). Approaches to address heteroscedasticity in time series analysis are beyond the scope of the present book.

The improvement of the model involving pulse intervention variables is also confirmed by the value of the Akaike information criterion which is equal to

$$\text{AIC} = \frac{1}{208}[-2(208)(3.305023) + 2(6+3)] = -6.5235.$$

This value implies that the model yields a better fit than the stochastic level and seasonal model without pulse intervention variables discussed in Section 4.4, even though two extra parameters are estimated in the present model.

8

General treatment of univariate state space models

This chapter provides a unified treatment of all univariate state space models, including those presented in Chapters 2–7. It also introduces a number of additional common features of state space methods not mentioned previously.

First, in Section 8.1 a general unified notation is presented for all univariate state space models. Then, alternative ways are discussed for handling explanatory and intervention variables in state space models in Section 8.2. In Section 8.3, the possibility of obtaining confidence intervals for all modelled state components is discussed. Next, the Kalman filter, as well as the concept of a filtered state, and prediction errors and their variances are introduced in Section 8.4. In Section 8.5, diagnostic tests are presented for testing the three basic assumptions of the distribution of residuals (independence, homoscedasticity, and normality), and for detecting structural breaks and outlier observations. Finally, Section 8.6 introduces the important issue of forecasting in time series analysis, while Section 8.7 illustrates how missing observations are handled in state space methods.

8.1. State space representation of univariate models*

All univariate state space models discussed in Chapters 2–7 can be expressed algebraically in one unified formulation. Using matrix algebra, all these models can be written in the following general format:

$$y_t = z_t' a_t + \varepsilon_t, \qquad\qquad \varepsilon_t \sim \text{NID}(0, \sigma_\varepsilon^2) \qquad\qquad (8.1)$$

$$a_{t+1} = T_t a_t + R_t \eta_t \qquad\qquad \eta_t \sim \text{NID}(0, Q_t) \qquad\qquad (8.2)$$

for $t = 1, \ldots, n$. The terms y_t and ε_t are still scalars (i.e. of order 1×1), as before. However, the remaining terms in (8.1) and (8.2) denote vectors and matrices. Specifically, z_t is an $m \times 1$ *observation* or *design* vector, T_t is an $m \times m$ *transition* matrix, a_t is an $m \times 1$ *state vector*, and m therefore denotes the number of elements in the state vector. In many state space models R_t in (8.2) is simply the identity matrix of order $m \times m$. However, in various models it is of order $m \times r$ with $r < m$, and consists of the first r columns of the identity matrix I_m. In this case R_t is called a *selection* matrix since it selects the rows of the state equation which have non-zero disturbance terms. Finally, the $r \times 1$ vector η_t contains the r state disturbances with zero means, and unknown variances collected in an $r \times r$ diagonal matrix Q_t. In this general formulation, equation (8.1) is called the *observation* or *measurement* equation, while equation (8.2) is called the *transition* or *state* equation.

By appropriate definitions of the vectors z_t, a_t, and η_t, and of the matrices T_t, R_t and Q_t, all the models discussed in Chapters 2–7 can be derived as special cases of (8.1) and (8.2). In this section, these definitions are provided for all the models discussed so far. In Section 8.2, matrix formulations (8.1) and (8.2) are used to present an alternative way of dealing with explanatory variables: by incorporating the regression coefficients in the state vector.

The local level model is the simplest special case of (8.1) and (8.2). Since the state vector of the local level model consists of only one element (i.e. the level), $m = 1$ in this case. Defining

$$a_t = \mu_t, \quad \eta_t = \xi_t, \quad z_t = T_t = R_t = 1, \quad Q_t = \sigma_\xi^2,$$

(all of order 1×1) for $t = 1, \ldots, n$, it is easily verified that (8.1) and (8.2) simplifies into the local level model which can be written as

$$y_t = \mu_t + \varepsilon_t, \quad \varepsilon_t \sim \text{NID}(0, \sigma_\varepsilon^2)$$
$$\mu_{t+1} = \mu_t + \xi_t, \quad \xi_t \sim \text{NID}(0, \sigma_\xi^2);$$

see also Chapter 2.

The local linear trend model of Chapter 3 requires a 2×1 state vector: one element for the level μ_t and one element for the slope v_t.

By defining

$$a_t = \begin{pmatrix} \mu_t \\ \nu_t \end{pmatrix}, \quad \eta_t = \begin{pmatrix} \xi_t \\ \zeta_t \end{pmatrix}, \quad T_t = \begin{bmatrix} 1 & 1 \\ 0 & 1 \end{bmatrix}, \quad Z_t = \begin{pmatrix} 1 \\ 0 \end{pmatrix},$$

$$Q_t = \begin{bmatrix} \sigma_\xi^2 & 0 \\ 0 & \sigma_\zeta^2 \end{bmatrix}, \quad \text{and} \quad R_t = \begin{bmatrix} 1 & 0 \\ 0 & 1 \end{bmatrix},$$

and for those familiar with matrix algebra, it is easily verified that the scalar notation of (8.1) and (8.2) leads to

$$y_t = \mu_t + \varepsilon_t, \qquad \varepsilon_t \sim \text{NID}(0, \sigma_\varepsilon^2)$$

$$\mu_{t+1} = \mu_t + \nu_t + \xi_t, \quad \xi_t \sim \text{NID}(0, \sigma_\xi^2)$$

$$\nu_{t+1} = \nu_t + \zeta_t, \qquad \zeta_t \sim \text{NID}(0, \sigma_\zeta^2)$$

which is the local linear trend model of Chapter 3.

The local level model can also be extended with a stochastic seasonal dummy effect, see Chapter 4. By defining

$$a_t = \begin{pmatrix} \mu_t \\ \gamma_{1,t} \\ \gamma_{2,t} \\ \gamma_{3,t} \end{pmatrix}, \quad \eta_t = \begin{pmatrix} \xi_t \\ \omega_t \end{pmatrix}, \quad T_t = \begin{bmatrix} 1 & 0 & 0 & 0 \\ 0 & -1 & -1 & -1 \\ 0 & 1 & 0 & 0 \\ 0 & 0 & 1 & 0 \end{bmatrix}, \quad Z_t = \begin{pmatrix} 1 \\ 1 \\ 0 \\ 0 \end{pmatrix},$$

$$Q_t = \begin{bmatrix} \sigma_\xi^2 & 0 \\ 0 & \omega_\zeta^2 \end{bmatrix}, \quad \text{and} \quad R_t = \begin{bmatrix} 1 & 0 \\ 0 & 1 \\ 0 & 0 \\ 0 & 0 \end{bmatrix},$$

and expanding (8.1) and (8.2) in scalar notation, we obtain

$$y_t = \mu_t + \gamma_{1,t} + \varepsilon_t, \qquad\qquad \varepsilon_t \sim \text{NID}(0, \sigma_\varepsilon^2)$$

$$\mu_{t+1} = \mu_t + \xi_t, \qquad\qquad \xi_t \sim \text{NID}(0, \sigma_\xi^2)$$

$$\gamma_{1,t+1} = -\gamma_{1,t} - \gamma_{2,t} - \gamma_{3,t} + \omega_t, \quad \omega_t \sim \text{NID}(0, \sigma_\omega^2)$$

$$\gamma_{2,t+1} = \gamma_{1,t},$$

$$\gamma_{3,t+1} = \gamma_{2,t},$$

which is the local level and dummy seasonal model for a quarterly time series, see Chapter 4.

Another extension of the local level model is considered in Chapter 5 and concerns the incorporation of explanatory effects. In the case of one regression variable, we have $y_t = \mu_t + \beta x_t + \epsilon_t$ and a state vector of two elements is required: one element for the level μ_t and one for the regression coefficient β. By the substitution of

$$a_t = \begin{pmatrix} \mu_t \\ \beta_t \end{pmatrix}, \quad \eta_t = \xi_t, \quad T_t = \begin{bmatrix} 1 & 0 \\ 0 & 1 \end{bmatrix}, \quad Z_t = \begin{pmatrix} 1 \\ x_t \end{pmatrix},$$

$$Q_t = \sigma_\xi^2, \quad \text{and} \quad R_t = \begin{bmatrix} 1 \\ 0 \end{bmatrix},$$

in (8.1) and (8.2), we obtain

$$y_t = \mu_t + \beta_t x_t + \varepsilon_t, \quad \varepsilon_t \sim \text{NID}(0, \sigma_\varepsilon^2)$$

$$\mu_{t+1} = \mu_t + \xi_t, \quad \xi_t \sim \text{NID}(0, \sigma_\xi^2)$$

$$\beta_{t+1} = \beta_t,$$

where $\beta = \beta_t = \beta_{t+1}$. This is the local level model with one deterministic explanatory variable x_t as discussed in Chapter 5.

In the same way, the local level model with an intervention variable of Chapter 6 has the matrix representation

$$a_t = \begin{pmatrix} \mu_t \\ \lambda_t \end{pmatrix}, \quad \eta_t = \xi_t, \quad T_t = \begin{bmatrix} 1 & 0 \\ 0 & 1 \end{bmatrix}, \quad Z_t = \begin{pmatrix} 1 \\ w_t \end{pmatrix},$$

$$Q_t = \sigma_\xi^2, \quad \text{and} \quad R_t = \begin{bmatrix} 1 \\ 0 \end{bmatrix},$$

for (8.1) and (8.2) that results in

$$y_t = \mu_t + \lambda_t w_t + \varepsilon_t, \quad \varepsilon_t \sim \text{NID}(0, \sigma_\varepsilon^2)$$

$$\mu_{t+1} = \mu_t + \xi_t, \quad \xi_t \sim \text{NID}(0, \sigma_\xi^2)$$

$$\lambda_{t+1} = \lambda_t,$$

where $\lambda = \lambda_t = \lambda_{t+1}$. This is the local level model with an intervention effect λw_t of Chapter 6.

For the seat belt model discussed in Chapter 7, we define

$$
a_t = \begin{pmatrix} \mu_t \\ \gamma_{1,t} \\ \gamma_{2,t} \\ \gamma_{3,t} \\ \beta_t \\ \lambda_t \end{pmatrix}, \quad \eta_t = \begin{pmatrix} \xi_t \\ \omega_t \end{pmatrix}, \quad T_t = \begin{bmatrix} 1 & 0 & 0 & 0 & 0 & 0 \\ 0 & -1 & -1 & -1 & 0 & 0 \\ 0 & 1 & 0 & 0 & 0 & 0 \\ 0 & 0 & 1 & 0 & 0 & 0 \\ 0 & 0 & 0 & 0 & 1 & 0 \\ 0 & 0 & 0 & 0 & 0 & 1 \end{bmatrix}, \quad z_t = \begin{pmatrix} 1 \\ 1 \\ 0 \\ 0 \\ x_t \\ w_t \end{pmatrix},
$$

$$
Q_t = \begin{bmatrix} \sigma_\xi^2 & 0 \\ 0 & \sigma_\omega^2 \end{bmatrix}, \quad \text{and} \quad R_t = \begin{bmatrix} 1 & 0 \\ 0 & 1 \\ 0 & 0 \\ 0 & 0 \\ 0 & 0 \\ 0 & 0 \end{bmatrix}.
$$

for (8.1) and (8.2). Expanding the matrix equations in scalar notation gives

$$y_t = \mu_t + \gamma_{1,t} + \beta_t x_t + \lambda_t w_t + \varepsilon_t, \qquad \varepsilon_t \sim \text{NID}(0, \sigma_\varepsilon^2)$$

$$\mu_{t+1} = \mu_t + \xi_t, \qquad \xi_t \sim \text{NID}(0, \sigma_\xi^2)$$

$$\gamma_{1,t+1} = -\gamma_{1,t} - \gamma_{2,t} - \gamma_{3,t} + \omega_t, \qquad \omega_t \sim \text{NID}(0, \sigma_\omega^2)$$

$$\gamma_{2,t+1} = \gamma_{1,t},$$

$$\gamma_{3,t+1} = \gamma_{2,t},$$

$$\beta_{t+1} = \beta_t,$$

$$\lambda_{t+1} = \lambda_t,$$

for $t = 1, \ldots, n$, which is the local level and dummy seasonal model for quarterly data together with a deterministic explanatory variable x_t and an intervention variable w_t.

In the next section and in Chapter 9, where multivariate state space models are introduced, we will use matrix formulation (8.1) and (8.2) more extensively.

State space models are typically called *time-invariant* when matrices T_t and Q_t, vector z_t and scalar σ_ε^2 in (8.1) and (8.2) do not change over time. Examples of time-invariant state space models are the local level model, the local linear trend model, and the local level and seasonal model. For these models the subscript t in T_t, Q_t, and z_t is redundant and may be dropped.

If one or more of these elements in (8.1) and (8.2) change over time, however, the corresponding model is said to be *time-varying*. Examples of time-varying models are, therefore, all state space models involving explanatory and/or intervention variables, since vector z_t then contains elements like x_t and/or w_t which do change over time.

The values of $\hat{y}_t = y_t - \epsilon_t = z_t' a_t$ in (8.1) (i.e., of y predicted in classical linear regression terms) are generically called the *signal*.

8.2. Incorporating regression effects*

Until now, the effects of explanatory and intervention variables on a time series were typically investigated by adding these variables to the *observation equation* (8.1) (see Chapters 5, 6, and 7). However, their effects can also be evaluated by adding them to the *state equation* (8.2). In this section we show how the vectors and matrices in (8.1) and (8.2) should be defined in order to achieve the latter effect, and how this alternative method relates to the previous one. To illustrate the two methods of handling explanatory variables, an explanatory variable will be added to the local linear trend model (see Chapter 3).

From Section 8.1 we have learned that the addition of an explanatory variable x_t to the observation equation (8.1) of the local linear trend model is achieved by defining

$$a_t = \begin{pmatrix} \mu_t \\ \nu_t \\ \beta_t \end{pmatrix}, \quad \eta_t = \begin{pmatrix} \xi_t \\ \zeta_t \end{pmatrix}, \quad T_t = \begin{bmatrix} 1 & 1 & 0 \\ 0 & 1 & 0 \\ 0 & 0 & 1 \end{bmatrix}, \quad z_t = \begin{pmatrix} 1 \\ 0 \\ x_t \end{pmatrix},$$

$$Q_t = \begin{bmatrix} \sigma_\xi^2 & 0 \\ 0 & \sigma_\zeta^2 \end{bmatrix}, \quad \text{and} \quad R_t = \begin{bmatrix} 1 & 0 \\ 0 & 1 \\ 0 & 0 \end{bmatrix}.$$

In scalar notation, we obtain the model

$$y_t = \mu_t + \beta_t x_t + \varepsilon_t, \quad \varepsilon_t \sim \text{NID}(0, \sigma_\varepsilon^2)$$

$$\mu_{t+1} = \mu_t + \nu_t + \xi_t, \quad \xi_t \sim \text{NID}(0, \sigma_\xi^2)$$

$$\nu_{t+1} = \nu_t + \zeta_t, \quad \zeta_t \sim \text{NID}(0, \sigma_\zeta^2)$$

$$\beta_{t+1} = \beta_t.$$

An explanatory variable x_t can also be incorporated in the *level equation* of the local linear trend model. We can achieve this by defining

$$a_t = \begin{pmatrix} \mu_t \\ \nu_t \\ \beta_t \end{pmatrix}, \quad \eta_t = \begin{pmatrix} \xi_t \\ \zeta_t \end{pmatrix}, \quad T_t = \begin{bmatrix} 1 & 1 & x_t \\ 0 & 1 & 0 \\ 0 & 0 & 1 \end{bmatrix}, \quad z_t = \begin{pmatrix} 1 \\ 0 \\ 0 \end{pmatrix},$$

$$Q_t = \begin{bmatrix} \sigma_\xi^2 & 0 \\ 0 & \sigma_\zeta^2 \end{bmatrix}, \quad \text{and} \quad R_t = \begin{bmatrix} 1 & 0 \\ 0 & 1 \\ 0 & 0 \end{bmatrix},$$

leading to the model equations

$$y_t = \mu_t + \varepsilon_t, \qquad \varepsilon_t \sim \text{NID}(0, \sigma_\varepsilon^2)$$
$$\mu_{t+1} = \mu_t + \nu_t + \beta_t x_t + \xi_t, \quad \xi_t \sim \text{NID}(0, \sigma_\xi^2)$$
$$\nu_{t+1} = \nu_t + \zeta_t, \qquad \zeta_t \sim \text{NID}(0, \sigma_\zeta^2)$$
$$\beta_{t+1} = \beta_t.$$

Further, by fixing all state disturbances in this model at zero, the recursive nature of the level equation implies the following classical regression model

$$y_t = \mu_1 + \nu_1(t-1) + \beta_1 \sum_{i=1}^{t-1} x_i + \varepsilon_t,$$

with

$$\sum_{i=1}^{t-1} x_i = 0 \text{ when } t = 1.$$

Thus, the effect of adding an explanatory variable to the level equation of a deterministic linear trend model is identical to regressing the dependent variable on two predictor variables: time, and the *cumulative sum* of the explanatory variable. If the level and slope components are treated stochastically, the regression coefficient β_1 still reflects the effect of the cumulative sum of the explanatory variable. When an explanatory variable x_t is added to the level equation, therefore, the regression coefficient is estimated differently than when x_t is included in the measurement equation.

This difference vanishes, however, when the explanatory variable is included *in first differences*, not *in levels*, in the level equation, that is

$$x_t^* = x_{t+1} - x_t,$$

(8.3)

and $x_n^* = 0$. The effect of (8.3) is that the original variable is transformed into its first differences, and that the whole resulting series is shifted back one point in time. By replacing x_t by x_t^* in the above definition of transition matrix T_t, the same results are obtained as when the original variable x_t is included in the observation equation. When dealing with a *level shift* intervention variable w_t (see Chapter 6), (8.3) effectively turns the level shift into a *pulse* but for one time point earlier in the series than the level shift.

When an explanatory or intervention variable is added to the measurement equation with the aim to influence the *slope* component of the model, then the *cumulative sum* $\sum_{i=1}^{t} x_i$ must be added to the measurement equation. Similarly, when adding an explanatory variable to the *slope equation* of the local linear trend model, we define

$$\alpha_t = \begin{pmatrix} \mu_t \\ \nu_t \\ \beta_t \end{pmatrix}, \quad \eta_t = \begin{pmatrix} \xi_t \\ \zeta_t \end{pmatrix}, \quad T_t = \begin{bmatrix} 1 & 1 & 0 \\ 0 & 1 & x_t \\ 0 & 0 & 1 \end{bmatrix}, \quad Z_t = \begin{pmatrix} 1 \\ 0 \\ 0 \end{pmatrix},$$

$$Q_t = \begin{bmatrix} \sigma_\xi^2 & 0 \\ 0 & \sigma_\zeta^2 \end{bmatrix}, \quad \text{and} \quad R_t = \begin{bmatrix} 1 & 0 \\ 0 & 1 \\ 0 & 0 \end{bmatrix},$$

and yield in scalar notation,

$$y_t = \mu_t + \varepsilon_t, \qquad \varepsilon_t \sim \text{NID}(0, \sigma_\varepsilon^2)$$

$$\mu_{t+1} = \mu_t + \nu_t + \xi_t, \qquad \xi_t \sim \text{NID}(0, \sigma_\xi^2)$$

$$\nu_{t+1} = \nu_t + \beta_t x_t + \zeta_t, \qquad \zeta_t \sim \text{NID}(0, \sigma_\zeta^2)$$

$$\beta_{t+1} = \beta_t.$$

By fixing all state disturbances in the latter model at zero and by expanding these equations, it is not very difficult to show that the following classical regression model is actually considered,

$$y_t = \mu_1 + \nu_1(t-1) + \beta_1 \sum_{i=1}^{t-1} \sum_{i=1}^{t-1} x_i + \varepsilon_t,$$

with

$$\sum_{i=1}^{t-1}\sum_{i=1}^{t-1} x_i = 0 \text{ when } t = 1, 2.$$

The explanatory variable passes through two recursions (i.e. the slope *and* the level equation). It follows that adding an explanatory variable x_t to the slope equation is equivalent to adding a *double cumulative sum* to the measurement equation. A different result is obtained compared to the inclusion of a (single) cumulative sum in the measurement equation. When adding an explanatory variable to the slope equation, therefore, the following *second differences* of the cumulative sum of the original variable x_t must be used

$$x_t^{**} = x_{t+2}^{***} - 2x_{t+1}^{***} + x_t^{***}, \tag{8.4}$$

with $x_t^{***} = \sum_{i=1}^{t} x_i$, and $x_t^{**} = 0$ for $t = n - 1, n$. When dealing with a slope shift intervention variable, x_t^{***} contains zeroes before the intervention and the values $1, 2, 3, 4, \ldots$ at and after the intervention. In that case, (8.4) effectively turns the slope shift into a pulse applied *two* time points earlier than the first non-zero value in x_t^{***}. For further details on handling explanatory and intervention variables in the state equation, we refer to Harvey (1989, Chapter 7).

8.3. Confidence intervals

In state space methods, the estimated state components discussed in Chapters 2–7 are associated with what are known as *estimation error variances*. Under the assumption of normality, this allows the construction of *confidence intervals* for each of the state components, thus allowing for an evaluation of the uncertainty in the modelled developments. As an example, again consider the time series analysis of the log of UK drivers KSI with the stochastic level and deterministic seasonal model discussed in Section 4.3. Figure 8.1 contains a plot of the estimation error variance corresponding to the stochastic level of this analysis. Note that the estimation error level variance, and therefore the uncertainty, is larger at the beginning and at the end of the series, as one would expect on intuitive grounds.

Letting $\text{Var}(\mu_t)$ denote the level estimation error variance displayed in Figure 8.1 for $t = 1, \ldots, n$, the 90% confidence limits of the stochastic level

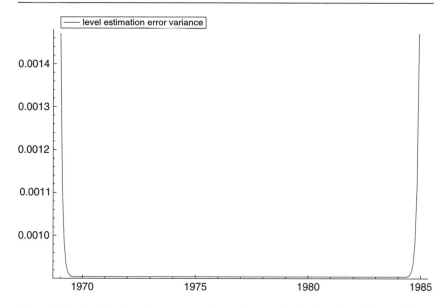

Figure 8.1. Level estimation error variance for stochastic level and deterministic seasonal model applied to the log of UK drivers KSI.

μ_t are computed by the well-known formula

$$\mu_t \pm 1.64\sqrt{\text{Var}(\mu_t)},$$

where $+1.64$ and -1.64 are the z-scores corresponding to the 90% interval around the mean of a normal distribution.

A plot of the obtained 90% confidence interval for the stochastic level is shown in Figure 8.2, together with the level itself as well as the observed values of the time series (see also Figure 4.6). Similarly, 90% confidence limits can be established for the deterministic seasonal, of which the last four years in the series are depicted in Figure 8.3.

Finally, the last four years of the 90% confidence limits for the combined prediction obtained by summing the stochastic level and deterministic seasonal are shown in Figure 8.4.

It is important to note that the appropriateness of the calculated confidence limits depends on whether the model residuals satisfy the assumptions of independence, homoscedasticity, and normality, as discussed in Chapter 2 and Section 8.5. If the first autocorrelation in the correlogram of the model residuals significantly deviates from zero and is positive, for example, then the estimation error variance of a state component will be

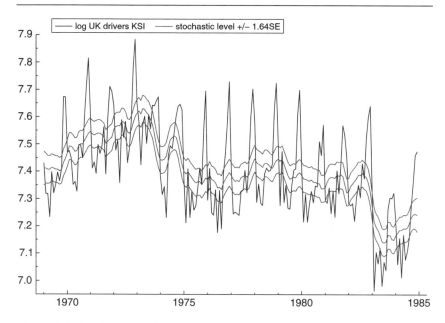

Figure 8.2. Stochastic level and its 90% confidence interval for stochastic level and deterministic seasonal model applied to the log of UK drivers KSI.

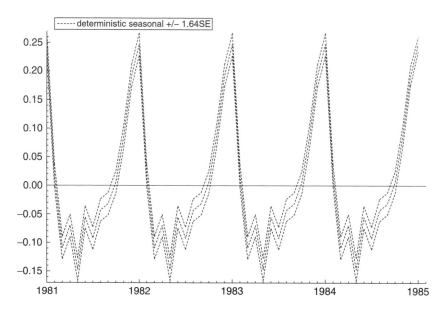

Figure 8.3. Deterministic seasonal and its 90% confidence interval for stochastic level and deterministic seasonal model applied to the log of UK drivers KSI.

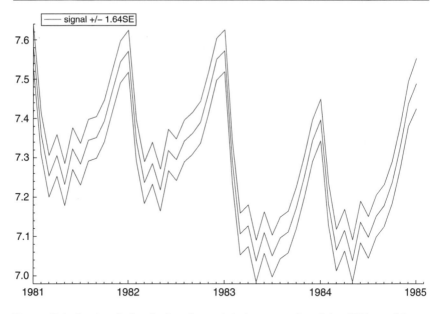

Figure 8.4. Stochastic level plus deterministic seasonal and its 90% confidence interval for stochastic level and deterministic seasonal model applied to the log of UK drivers KSI.

too small, and the estimated boundaries of the confidence interval will also be too small.

8.4. Filtering and prediction

In time series analysis by state space methods, the state components can be estimated in different ways. Throughout Chapters 2–7, and in Section 8.3, we have presented the *smoothed state*. This is the smoothed estimate of the state vector for which all observations are used. The *filtered state* is the estimate of the state vector based on all past observations and the current observations. The *predicted state* is based on only the past observations. In this section we explore the different estimates of the state vector further. The state estimates are considered for given values of hyperparameters (i.e. the variances of the irregular and of the state disturbances) and for given initial values of the state components. The estimations of the state vector are carried out by performing two passes through the data:

1. a *forward* pass, from $t = 1, \ldots, n$, using a recursive algorithm known as the *Kalman filter* that is applied to the observed time series;

2. a *backward* pass from $t = n, \ldots, 1$, using recursive algorithms known as *state and disturbance smoothers* that are applied to the output of the Kalman filter.

The forward pass through the data with the well-known Kalman (1960) filter provides all the estimates that are relevant for the predicted or filtered state. In the case of filtering, these estimates include the filtered state and the filtered state estimation error variances. The variances are useful for the construction of confidence limits in the same ways as for the smoothed state in Section 8.3. In the case of prediction, the observation prediction errors and their variances are of particular interest, see below. The main purpose of the Kalman filter is to obtain optimal values of the state at time point t, *only* considering the observations $\{y_1, y_2, \ldots, y_{t-1}\}$. A key property of the predicted state and its related estimates is therefore that they are only based on *past values* of the observed time series.

The backward pass through the data is only required for smoothing that leads to estimates such as the smoothed states and smoothed disturbances. Smoothing also produces the smoothed state estimation error variances (see Section 8.3), the smoothed irregular component and the smoothed state disturbances and their variances (see Chapters 2–7). The main purpose of state and disturbance smoothing is to obtain estimated values of the state and disturbance vectors at time point t, considering *all* available observations $\{y_1, y_2, \ldots, y_n\}$.

In Figure 8.5 both versions of the state are displayed for the local level model applied to the Norwegian road traffic fatalities series discussed in Section 2.3. As Figure 8.5 points out, and for reasons that will be explained below, the changes in the filtered state always lag one time point (in this example: one year) behind the changes in the smoothed state.

Letting a_t denote the Kalman filtered state at time point t, the central formula in the recursive Kalman filter updating scheme is:

$$a_{t+1} = a_t + K_t(y_t - z_t' a_t). \tag{8.5}$$

For the local level model, (8.5) simplifies into

$$a_{t+1} = a_t + K_t(y_t - a_t). \tag{8.6}$$

Figure 8.6 illustrates two steps of the Kalman filter process (8.6) for the local level model applied to the time series discussed in Section 2.3. For a better understanding of the Kalman updating process, the figure only

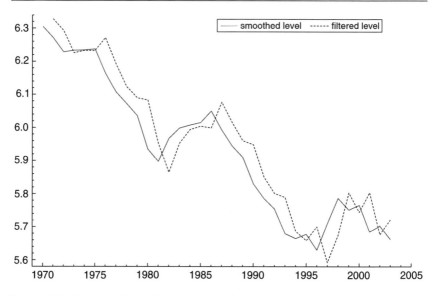

Figure 8.5. Smoothed and filtered state of the local level model applied to Norwegian road traffic fatalities.

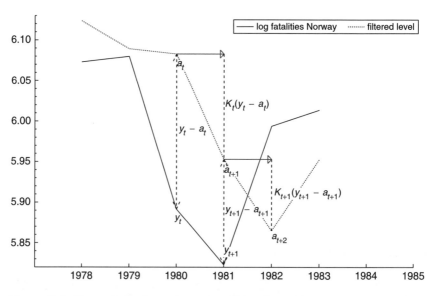

Figure 8.6. Illustration of computation of the filtered state for the local level model applied to Norwegian road traffic fatalities.

displays that part of the observed time series and of the filtered state (here one-dimensional since the state only contains the level) corresponding to the years 1978 through 1983.

Picking up the Kalman filter process at time point $t = 1980$, the current value of the filtered level based on all past observations $\{y_{1970}, y_{1971}, \ldots, y_{1979}\}$ of the log of Norwegian road traffic fatalities in Figure 8.5 is a_t (i.e. a_{1980}). Now, suppose that the value of y_t were unknown (because the time series had only been observed up to y_{1979} for example, or because information on y_{1980} happened to be missing). Lacking new information about the observed time series, and since the value of the filtered state a_{1980} represents all that could be learned from the past observations $\{y_{1970}, y_{1971}, \ldots, y_{1979}\}$, the best option would simply be to move the filtered state forward unchanged. In the absence of new data, therefore, the best *prediction* of the filtered state at time point $(t + 1)$ would simply be to have $a_{t+1} = a_t$, or in this case $a_{1981} = a_{1980}$. Since a_t only consists of a level component in the present example, in Figure 8.6 this prediction is indicated by the horizontal arrow extending from a_t. However, since the value for y_t (i.e. of y_{1980}) is known in the present situation, the latter value can be fed into the Kalman filter (8.6), and the discrepancy between y_t and a_t in 1980 (i.e. the vertical double arrow labelled $y_t - a_t$ in Figure 8.6) is used to *update* the estimate for a_t in 1980, yielding the value labelled a_{t+1} for 1981 in the figure. Since the discrepancy $y_t - a_t$ is negative in this case, the update a_{t+1} in Figure 8.5 results in a *decrease* of the filtered level.

In the next step of the filter (8.6), if information on y_{1981} is not available, the best estimate for a_{1982} is the current best estimate a_{1981}. This corresponds to the horizontal arrow at a_{t+1} in Figure 8.6. Since the value of y_{1981} happens to be available in the present case, the discrepancy between y_{1981} and a_{1981} (the vertical double arrow labelled $y_{t+1} - a_{t+1}$ in Figure 8.6) can be used to update the state in 1982, yielding the value labelled a_{t+2} in the figure. Since the update of the filtered state at time point $(t + 1)$ is based on the difference between y_t and a_t at time point t, the update a_{t+1} always lags one observation. This can be clearly seen in Figure 8.5.

Letting $v_t = y_t - a_t$ for $t = 1, \ldots, n$, the values of v_t are called the *one-step ahead prediction errors* or the *forecast (or prediction) errors*, since they quantify the lack of accuracy of a_t in predicting the observed value of y_t at time point t. The prediction errors are also denoted as *innovations* because they bring in new information, thus allowing the system to adapt itself to the new incoming information. The top of Figure 8.7 displays all the prediction errors v_t obtained in the analysis of the Norwegian fatalities, two of which were already shown in Figure 8.6.

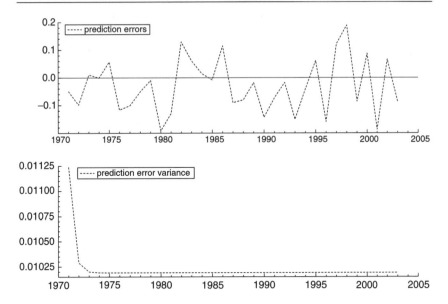

Figure 8.7. One-step ahead prediction errors (top) and their variances (bottom) for the local level model applied to Norwegian road traffic fatalities.

The value of K_t in (8.6), which is a scalar in the local level model, typically determines *how much* the prediction error at time point t is allowed to influence the estimate of the state at time point $(t + 1)$. The larger the value of K_t, the larger the impact v_t will have on the next filtered state. The value of K_t is therefore called the Kalman *gain* and can be interpreted as a simultaneous compromise between the (un)certainty of two issues, all rolled into one. When the uncertainty of the state based on past observations $\{y_1, y_2, \ldots, y_{t-1}\}$ is large (relative to the uncertainty of the new observation y_t), then the value of K_t will tend to *one*, allowing the newly incoming information y_t to have a large impact on the next value of the state. At the same time, when the uncertainty of the new observation y_t is large (relative to the uncertainty based on the past observations $\{y_1, y_2, \ldots, y_{t-1}\}$), then the value of K_t will tend to *zero, disallowing* the newly incoming information y_t to have much impact on the next value of the state. When both (un)certainties cancel each other out, this is typically reflected in a value of 0.5 for the Kalman gain.

The value of K_t is equal to P_t/F_t, where P_t denotes the filtered state estimation error variance, and F_t the variance of the one-step prediction errors v_t. The prediction error variances corresponding to the analysis of the Norwegian fatalities are displayed at the bottom of Figure 8.7.

As Figure 8.7 shows, the prediction error variances (sometimes abbreviated as PEV in the literature on state space methods) are monotonically decreasing with time. Moreover, for time-invariant models, the prediction error variance converges to a constant value. These properties also apply to the filtered state estimation error variances P_t. This means that the Kalman gain K_t (being the ratio of P_t and F_t) also converges to a constant value. This simplifies the computations in the Kalman filter (8.6) after convergence to what is called *a steady state*.

The prediction errors v_t and their variances F_t also play a key role in the maximisation of the log-likelihood function in state space methods. For univariate state space models the diffuse log-likelihood is defined as:

$$\log L_d = -\frac{n}{2}\log(2\pi) - \frac{1}{2}\sum_{t=d+1}^{n}\left(\log F_t + \frac{v_t^2}{F_t}\right), \tag{8.7}$$

where d is the number of diffuse initial elements of the state. It follows from (8.7) that the value of the log-likelihood function is maximised by simultaneously *minimising* the prediction errors v_t and their variances F_t. Unlike classical regression, therefore, in state space methods the (hyper)parameter estimates are obtained by minimising the *prediction* errors v_t and their variances F_t, not by minimising the *observation* errors or disturbances ε_t and their variance σ_ε^2.

The maximisation of the likelihood is based for an important part on the minimisation of the prediction or one-step ahead forecast error. Given the model structure, we aim to find those parameters that weight the past observations in an optimal way in order to provide the best prediction of the current observation. This is somewhat different than classical regression where issues like 'past' and 'future' play no role.

This also explains why the stochastic level and deterministic seasonal models applied to the log UK drivers KSI series (as discussed in Sections 4.3 and 7.3) result in a better fit according to the Akaike information criterion (which is based on the value of log-likelihood function (8.7)) than the local level model discussed in Section 2.2, even though the observation errors or disturbances are *smaller* for the latter model (see Figure 2.4) than for the former models (see Figures 4.9 and 7.4).

The prediction errors v_t (and their variances F_t) are further instrumental in establishing whether the residuals of a state space model are independently, identically, and normally distributed (as will be discussed in the next section), while the Kalman filter can be used to extrapolate time series observations into the unknown future (see Section 8.6).

8.5. Diagnostic tests

All significance tests in linear Gaussian models are based on three assumptions concerning the residuals of the analysis. These residuals should satisfy the following three properties, which are listed here in decreasing order of importance:

1. independence;
2. homoscedasticity;
3. normality.

In this section tests are discussed that can be used to establish whether the residuals of state space methods satisfy these three assumptions. In state space methods, these tests are applied to what are known as the *standardised prediction errors*, which are defined as

$$e_t = \frac{v_t}{\sqrt{F_t}}. \tag{8.8}$$

For the definitions of v_t and F_t in (8.8), we refer to Section 8.4. It follows from (8.8) that the *variance* of the standardised prediction errors is approximately equal to one.

The diagnostic tests will be illustrated with the standardised prediction errors (8.8) obtained wih the combined descriptive and explanatory model applied to the UK drivers KSI series in Section 7.3. A graph of the standardised prediction errors (8.8) of this analysis is shown in Figure 8.8. Note that the residuals corresponding to $t = 1, \ldots, 14$ are not plotted in the figure, nor are they used in the diagnostic tests, because they correspond to the 14 diffuse initial state values which need to be estimated for the level, the seasonal, and the intervention and explanatory variable components in model (7.1) (see Section 7.3).

We start with the first and most important assumption: *independence*. The assumption of independence of the residuals can be checked with the Box–Ljung statistic. Letting

$$r_k = \frac{\sum_{t=1}^{n-k} (e_t - \bar{e})(e_{t+k} - \bar{e})}{\sum_{t=1}^{n} (e_t - \bar{e})^2}$$

denote the residual autocorrelation for lag k, where $\bar{e}$ is the mean of the n residuals, the Box–Ljung statistic is defined as

$$Q(k) = n(n+2) \sum_{l=1}^{k} \frac{r_l^2}{n-l},$$

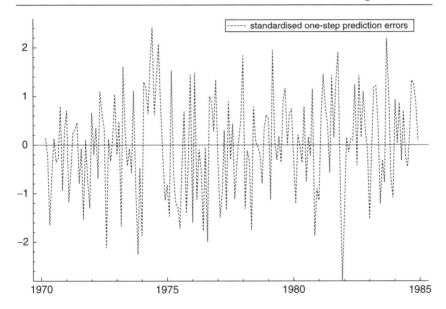

Figure 8.8. Standardised one-step prediction errors of model in Section 7.3.

for lags $l = 1, \ldots, k$. Since there are $n = 192 - 14 = 178$ residuals in Figure 8.8, and because the values of the autocorrelations of the residuals at lags 1 through 10 (see Figure 8.9) are 0.078, 0.070, −0.062, −0.108, 0.062, 0.00018, 0.0050, −0.164, −0.0589, and −0.114, respectively, the Box–Ljung statistic for the first 10 lags equals

$$Q(10) = (178)(180) \left(\frac{0.078^2}{178 - 1} + \frac{0.070^2}{178 - 2} + \frac{(-0.062)^2}{178 - 3} + \cdots + \frac{(-0.114)^2}{178 - 10} \right)$$
$$= 13.719.$$

Thus, for the first 10 autocorrelations $Q(10) = 13.719$. This should be tested against a χ^2-distribution with $(k - w + 1)$ degrees of freedom, where w is the number of estimated hyperparameters (i.e. disturbance variances). In the present case there are $(k - w + 1) = (10 - 2 + 1) = 9$ degrees of freedom, and the critical value at the 5% level in the latter distribution equals 16.92. Since the observed value of $Q(10)$ satisfies

$$Q(k) < \chi^2_{(k-w+1;0.05)},$$

the null hypothesis of independence is not rejected, and there is no reason to assume that the residuals in Figure 8.8 are serially correlated.

The second most important assumption is *homoscedasticity* of the residuals. Homoscedasticity of the residuals can be checked with the following

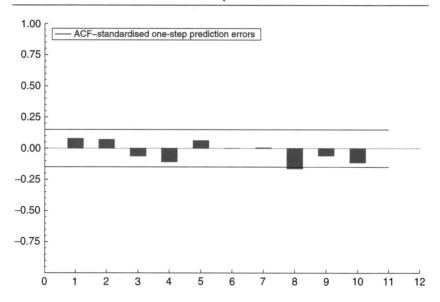

Figure 8.9. Correlogram of standardised one-step prediction errors in Figure 8.8, first 10 lags.

test statistic:

$$H(h) = \frac{\sum_{t=n-h+1}^{n} e_t^2}{\sum_{t=d+1}^{d+h} e_t^2}$$

where d is the number of diffuse initial elements, and h is the nearest integer to $(n-d)/3$. The statistic therefore tests whether the variance of the residuals in the first third part of the series is equal to the variance of the residuals corresponding to the last third part of the series. This typically calls for a two-tailed test. For the analysis discussed in Section 7.3, the integer nearest to $(n-d)/3 = (192-14)/3 = 59.33$ is $h = 59$, and the value of the test statistic equals

$$H(59) = \frac{\sum_{t=133}^{192} e_t^2}{\sum_{t=15}^{73} e_t^2} = 1.0248.$$

This should be tested against an F-distribution with (h, h) degrees of freedom. Applying the usual 5% rule for rejection of the null hypothesis of equal variances, for a two-tailed test we must find the critical values corresponding to the upper and lower 2.5% in the two tails of the F-distribution. If $H(h)$ is larger than 1, it is enough to check whether $H(h) < F(h, h; 0.025)$. On the other hand, if $H(h)$ is smaller than 1 we have to use the *reciprocal* of $H(h)$, and check whether $1/H(h) < F(h, h; 0.025)$.

Since $H(59) > 1$ in the present case and $H(59) < F(59, 59; 0.025)$, the null hypothesis of equal variances is not rejected, and there is no reason to assume departure from homoscedasticity for the residuals in Figure 8.8.

The least important assumption is that the residuals are *normally distributed*. Normality of the residuals can be checked with the following test statistic:

$$N = n \left(\frac{S^2}{6} + \frac{(K-3)^2}{24} \right),$$

with

$$S = \frac{\frac{1}{n} \sum_{t=1}^{n} (e_t - \bar{e})^3}{\sqrt{\left(\frac{1}{n} \sum_{t=1}^{n} (e_t - \bar{e})^2 \right)^3}}, \qquad K = \frac{\frac{1}{n} \sum_{t=1}^{n} (e_t - \bar{e})^4}{\left(\frac{1}{n} \sum_{t=1}^{n} (e_t - \bar{e})^2 \right)^2},$$

where S denotes the skewness of the residuals, and K the kurtosis. In the present example,

$$S = \frac{-0.11213}{\sqrt{(0.99505)^3}} = -0.11297, \qquad K = \frac{2.5952}{0.99505^2} = 2.6211,$$

and

$$N = 178 \left(\frac{(-0.11297)^2}{6} + \frac{(2.6211 - 3)^2}{24} \right) = 1.4435.$$

This should be tested against a χ^2-distribution with two degrees of freedom. Since the critical value at the 5% level in the latter distribution equals 5.99, and the observed value of N satisfies

$$N < \chi^2_{(2;0.05)},$$

the null hypothesis of normality is not rejected, and there is no reason to assume that the residuals in Figure 8.8 are not normally distributed (see also Figure 8.10).

A second important diagnostic tool for determining the appropriateness of a model is provided by the inspection of what are known as the *auxiliary residuals*. As already mentioned in Section 8.4, the disturbance smoothing filters applied in the backward pass through the data yield, amongst others, estimates of the smoothed observation and state disturbances, and of their variances. The auxiliary residuals are obtained by dividing the smoothed disturbances with the square root of their corresponding variances, as follows:

$$\frac{\hat{\epsilon}_t}{\sqrt{\text{Var}(\hat{\epsilon}_t)}}, \quad \text{and} \quad \frac{\hat{\eta}_t}{\sqrt{\text{Var}(\hat{\eta}_t)}},$$

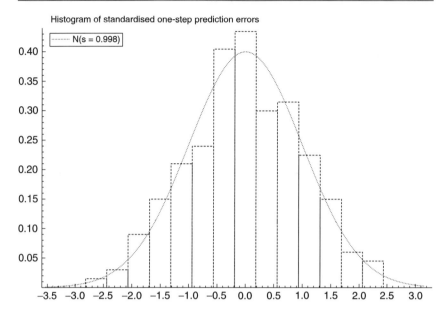

Figure 8.10. Histogram of standardised one-step prediction errors in Figure 8.8.

for $t = 1, \ldots, n$, resulting in *standardised* smoothed disturbances. Inspection of the standardised smoothed observation disturbances allows the detection of possible *outlier* observations in a time series, while the inspection of the standardised smoothed state disturbances makes it possible to detect *structural breaks* in the underlying development of a time series.

As an example, consider the stochastic level and deterministic seasonal model applied to the UK drivers KSI series (see Section 4.3). The standardised smoothed level disturbances of this analysis are presented at the top of Figure 8.11, while the standardised smoothed observation disturbances are shown at the bottom of the same figure.

Each of the auxiliary residuals at the top of Figure 8.11 can be considered as a t-test for the null hypothesis that there was no structural break in the level of the observed time series. Applying the usual 95% confidence limits of ± 1.96 corresponding to a two-tailed t-test (shown in the figure as two straight horizontal lines), we see that possible structural level breaks occurred at five time points. This is less than the $n/20 = 192/20 = 9.6 \approx 10$ time points expected to exceed the 95% confidence limits, purely based on chance. Even so, the auxiliary residual for January 1983 at the top of Figure 8.11 particularly stands out as being located far outside the 95% confidence limits.

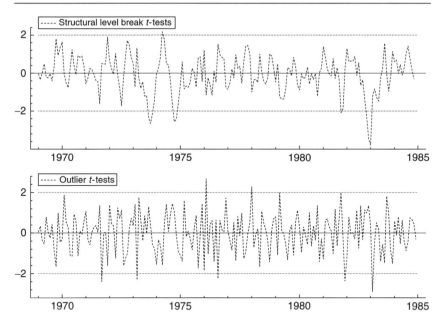

Figure 8.11. Standardised smoothed level disturbances (top) and standardised smoothed observation disturbances (bottom) for analysis of UK drivers KSI in Section 4.3.

Analogously, each of the auxiliary residuals at the bottom of Figure 8.11 can also be considered as a *t*-test, but now for the null hypothesis that the corresponding observation in the time series is *not* an outlier. Since only seven out of the 192 standardised smoothed observation disturbances exceed the confidence limits, while we would expect only 10 of them to exceed the confidence limits according to chance (see above), and since, moreover, none of them are extreme, we conclude that the series does not contain outlier observations.

If an outlier is detected the first thing to do is to check the value of the corresponding observation in the time series for possible measurement or typing errors, and then correct the value accordingly. If the value seems appropriate, on the other hand, then the outlier observation can be handled by adding a *pulse* intervention variable to the model, consisting of a one at the time point corresponding to the outlier observation, and zeroes elsewhere (see Section 7.4 for an example). A structural break in the *level* is typically handled by adding a *level shift* intervention variable to the model (see also Chapter 6 and Section 8.2).

However, care should be taken not to indiscriminately add pulse and/or level shift intervention variables for each and every outlier and structural break detected in the auxiliary residuals. First of all, although the addition of pulse intervention variables for each outlier observation may well improve the fit of the model, it may also result in an equally false sense of confidence in the *forecasts* obtained from a thus improved model (see also Section 8.6). Second, the insertion of an intervention variable as the result of an observed structural break in the auxiliary residuals should always be based on a *theory* concerning the possible *cause* of the structural break.

In the present case the extreme value of the auxiliary residual observed in January 1983 at the top of Figure 8.11 coincides with an actual outside event in the United Kingdom: the introduction of legislation from February 1983 onwards that obliges motor vehicle drivers and front seat passengers to wear a seat belt.

Since the introduction of this important road traffic safety measure was neglected in the analysis of Section 4.3, this clearly shows up as a large standardised level disturbance at the top of Figure 8.11.

Adding a level shift intervention variable for the introduction of the seat belt law in February 1983 to the stochastic level and deterministic seasonal model (see Section 7.3) yields the standardised smoothed level disturbances shown at the top of Figure 8.12, and the standardised observation disturbances displayed at the bottom of Figure 8.12.

In this case, the theory is that the structural level break was caused by the introduction of the seat belt law. This theory is not only confirmed by the significant value of the regression coefficient corresponding to the intervention variable (indicating a 21% decrease in the number of UK drivers KSI, as discussed in Section 7.3), but also by the disappearance of the large auxiliary residual in January 1983 (see the plot displayed at the top of Figure 8.12). For a detailed investigation of the properties of auxiliary residuals, we refer to Harvey and Koopman (1992).

8.6. Forecasting

In state space methods it is easy to compute the forecasts of a time series. They are simply obtained by continuing the Kalman filter (8.5) after the end of the observed time series. As already mentioned in Section 8.4 for the local level model, in the absence of new observations the best option is to move the filtered state forward *as is*. When we arrive at the end of a

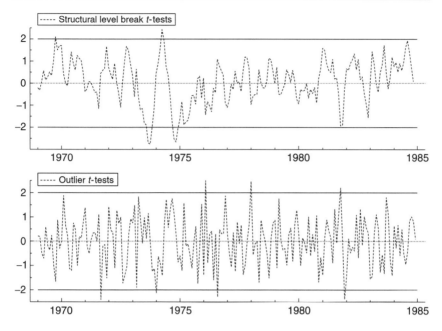

Figure 8.12. Standardised smoothed level disturbances (top) and standardised smoothed observation disturbances (bottom) for analysis of UK drivers KSI in Section 7.3.

series, the update of the filtered state at time point $t = n$ equals

$$a_n = a_{n-1} + K_{n-1}(y_{n-1} - z'_{n-1}a_{n-1}),$$ (8.9)

(see (8.5)). At this point there is still one observation left which has not yet been used in the Kalman filter updating process. This is the last observation y_n of the series. This last observation can be used to update the filtered state at time point $t = n + 1$, as follows:

$$a_{n+1} = a_n + K_n(y_n - z'_n a_n).$$ (8.10)

Now, all the available information in the series has been used, and from $n + 1$ onwards the filtered state no longer changes. Letting $\bar{a}_{n+1} = a_{n+1}$, the forecasts are simply obtained from

$$\bar{a}_{n+1+j} = \bar{a}_{n+j},$$ (8.11)

for $j = 1, \ldots, J - 1$, where J (the number of time points for which forecasts are calculated) is called the *lead time*. It may be noted that the same values are obtained by continuing the Kalman filter recursions (8.5) provided that we set $v_{n+j} = 0$ and $K_{n+j} = 0$ for $j = 1, \ldots, J - 1$.

Forecasts are useful not only because they provide information on future developments based on the past, but also because they make it possible to investigate whether data that become newly available in a series behave according to expectation or not. We present three examples of forecasting. The third and last example is an application of forecasting that combines both aspects in the same way as has been discussed in Harvey and Durbin (1986). The first two examples present forecasts obtained with the local level model, and with the smooth trend model (see Chapter 2 and Section 3.4).

The analysis of the log of the annual number of traffic fatalities in Norway (see Section 2.3) was used to obtain forecasts for the series using a lead time of five years. The observations of the series are shown in Figure 8.13, together with the filtered level and the forecasted values for the years 2004–2008. When the local level model is used for forecasting, the forecasts are always located on a straight horizontal line whose level is equal to the filtered level at $t = n + 1$. This is in complete agreement with the fact that for a correctly specified model the best source of information for the future is the filtered state at $t = n + 1$, since this time point contains

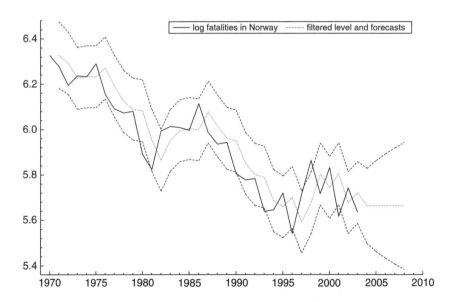

Figure 8.13. Filtered level, and five year forecasts for Norwegian fatalities, including their 90% confidence interval.

the most updated information concerning the past observations of the series. In the present case, the value of the level at $t = n + 1$ equals 5.6627. Since the dependent variable is analysed in its logarithm, the forecasted values imply that there will be a constant number of $e^{5.6627} = 288$ road traffic fatalities per year in Norway in the years 2004–2008.

Forecasts are, by their very nature, bound to be subject to more uncertainty than any estimated value falling within the time range of the observed time series. It is therefore customary to be somewhat less conservative than usual in setting up the confidence limits of forecasted values. Instead of the usual 95% values, for forecasts confidence limits of 90% or 85%, or even lower are often used. In Figure 8.13 the 90% confidence interval has been used, which is computed as

$$a_t \pm 1.64\sqrt{P_t},$$

where a_t is the filtered level and P_t is the filtered level estimation error variance (see also Section 8.4). Note that the uncertainty of the estimated forecasts quickly increases with time.

The forecasts obtained with the smooth trend model applied to the log of the annual number of traffic fatalities in Finland (see Section 3.4) are shown in Figure 8.14, including their 90% confidence interval. When the

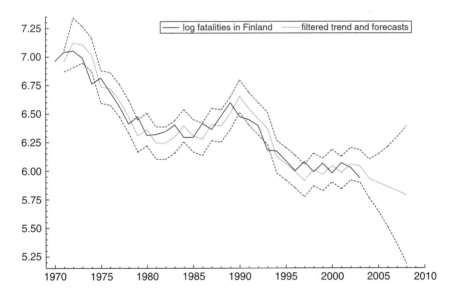

Figure 8.14. Filtered trend, and five-year forecasts for Finnish fatalities, including their 90% confidence limits.

local linear trend model is used for forecasting, from $t = n + 1$ onwards the forecasts always are located on a straight line with constant level and slope. The values of the forecasts are 5.9332, 5.8976, 5.8620, 5.8264, and 5.7908, respectively. In terms of absolute numbers, this means that the predicted numbers of road traffic fatalities in Finland are 377, 364, 351, 339, and 327 for the years 2004, 2005, 2006, 2007, and 2008, respectively.

As a last example, the first 169 time points of the log of the numbers of UK drivers KSI before the introduction of the seat belt law are analysed first. Then, forecasts of the latter analysis are determined and compared with the actual development in the number of drivers KSI after the introduction of the seat belt law in the UK in February 1983. The idea is that, if the forecasted values from the analysis up till February 1983 are (very) different from the actual and/or modelled values after the introduction of the seat belt law, this provides additional confirmation of the effect of this law.

Time series analysis of the first 169 time points in the series (up to February 1983) of the log of the numbers of drivers KSI with a stochastic level and seasonal model, and including the log of petrol price as an explanatory variable, yields the following results:

```
it0    f=    0.7926428
it5    f=    0.8010981
it10   f=    0.8029273
it15   f=    0.8927482
it20   f=    0.9535592
it25   f=    0.9552286
it30   f=    0.9556553
it34   f=    0.9556575
Strong convergence
```

The estimated value of the regression weight for the log of petrol price is equal to -0.29506 for $t = 1, \ldots, 169$, which is associated with an elasticity value of 0.295%. The Akaike information criterion for this model equals

$$ \text{AIC} = \frac{1}{169} [-2(169)(0.9556575) + 2(13 + 3)] = -1.72197. $$

Since the variance of the seasonal disturbances is almost zero, the analysis is repeated with a deterministic seasonal yielding the following results.

```
it0    f=    0.9455970
it1    f=    0.9470922
it2    f=    0.9502790
it3    f=    0.9534790
it4    f=    0.9553035
it5    f=    0.9555801
it6    f=    0.9555823
it7    f=    0.9555823
Strong convergence
```

In this case, the estimated value of the regression weight for the log of petrol price equals -0.29212 for $t = 1, \ldots, 169$. In the present analysis, the estimated variance of the observation disturbances is 0.00414 and the estimated variance of the level disturbances equals 0.000253.

Note the close similarity between these parameter estimates and those obtained with the analysis of the complete series. For the complete series, the estimated variances are 0.00403 and 0.000268, respectively, and the regression weight for the log of petrol price is -0.27674 (see Section 7.3).

The Akaike information criterion for the stochastic level and deterministic seasonal model applied to the first 169 observations of the UK drivers KSI series equals

$$\text{AIC} = \frac{1}{169} \left[-2(169)(0.9555823) + 2(13 + 2) \right] = -1.73365.$$

The latter AIC is slightly smaller than the previous one, meaning that the second model results in a slightly better fit to the data.

Therefore, the second model was used to calculate forecasts for the next 23 time points in the series (i.e. for $t = 170, \ldots, 192$). In these calculations the observed values of the log of petrol price for $t = 170, \ldots, 192$ were used, but not those for the log of the number of drivers KSI. The forecasted values for the log of the number of drivers KSI for $t = 170, \ldots, 192$ (i.e. for February 1983 up to and including December 1984) are shown in Figure 8.15.

In Figure 8.15 the 90% confidence limits for the 23 forecasted values are also displayed. As can be seen in the latter figure, the confidence limits become larger and larger as the forecasts are for observations further into the future. This is as one would expect on intuitive grounds.

Figure 8.16 contains the last three years of the observed log of the number of drivers KSI, together with the forecasts from Figure 8.15, and the modelled complete series including an intervention variable for the introduction of the seat belt law (see also Section 7.3). Figure 8.16 provides confirmation of the effect of this law, since the predicted values of the series including the intervention variable are very similar to the observed values from February 1983 onwards, whereas the 23 forecasted values from Figure 8.15 are all much larger than the observed values.

It may finally be noted that the results reported here are slightly different from the results obtained in Harvey and Durbin (1986). The reason for the difference is twofold. First, Harvey and Durbin used a slightly different dummy variable for modelling the intervention effect in the complete series. They coded the dummy variable as 0.18 in January 1983,

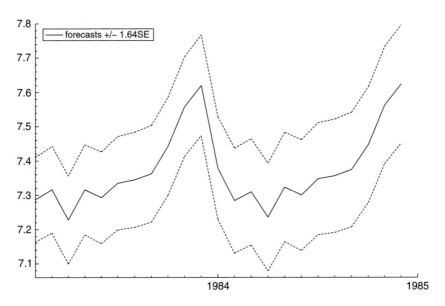

Figure 8.15. Forecasts for $t = 170, \ldots, 192$ including their 90% confidence interval.

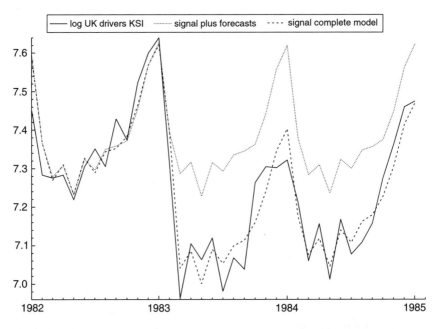

Figure 8.16. Last four years (1981–1984) in the time series of the log of numbers of drivers KSI: observed series, forecasts obtained from the analysis up to February 1983, and modelled development for the complete series including an intervention variable for February 1983.

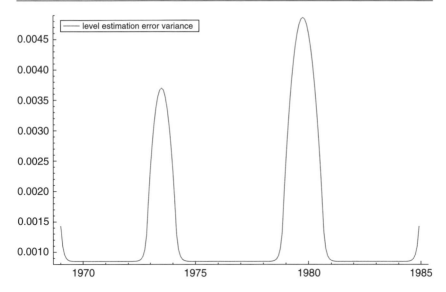

Figure 8.17. Stochastic level estimation error variance for log drivers KSI with observations at $t = 48, \ldots, 62$ and $t = 120, \ldots, 140$ treated as missing.

while here the dummy variable was coded zero at this time point. Second, Harvey and Durbin fixed the observation and state error variances in the analysis of the complete series on the values obtained in the analysis of the series up till February 1983. Here these variances were re-estimated in the analysis of the complete series containing the intervention variable.

8.7. Missing observations

In state space methods, missing observations in a time series are easily dealt with. As an example, the log of the UK drivers KSI were re-analysed using a stochastic level and deterministic seasonal model (see also Section 4.3), but now treating the observations at time points $t = 48$ through 62, and at time points $t = 120$ through 140 as missing.

The analysis of the $(192 - 15 - 21) = 156$ remaining non-missing observations leads to a level estimation error variance that is shown in Figure 8.17. As discussed in Section 8.3, this variance can be used to construct confidence intervals for the level component. The stochastic level and its 90% confidence interval are displayed in Figure 8.18, together with the 156 available observations.

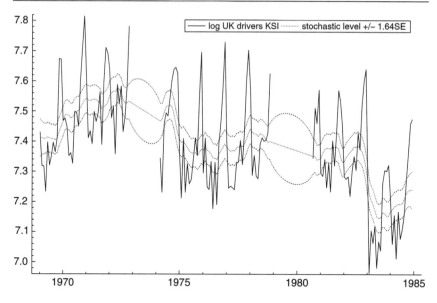

Figure 8.18. Stochastic level and its 90% confidence interval for log drivers KSI with observations at $t = 48, \ldots, 62$ and $t = 120, \ldots, 140$ treated as missing.

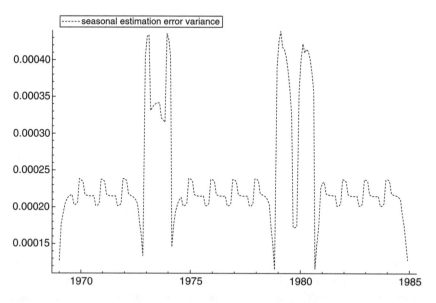

Figure 8.19. Seasonal estimation error variance for log drivers KSI with observations missing at $t = 48, \ldots, 62$ and $t = 120, \ldots, 140$.

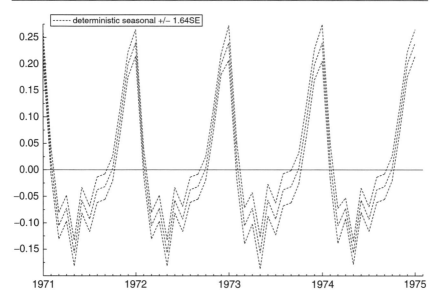

Figure 8.20. Deterministic seasonal and its 90% confidence interval for $t = 25, \ldots, 72$.

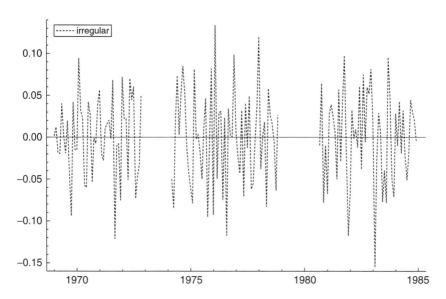

Figure 8.21. Irregular component.

Figures 8.17 and 8.18 nicely reflect that the uncertainty in the modelled level is larger at the time points for which no observations are available, as would be expected intuitively.

Figure 8.19 is the estimation error variance for the deterministic seasonal, while Figure 8.20 shows part of the seasonal (for $t = 25, \ldots, 72$) and the 90% confidence interval. As both figures illustrate, the seasonal variance and confidence interval are larger for time points corresponding to missing observations.

Figure 8.21 shows the irregular resulting from the analysis of an incomplete time series.

Finally, it is interesting to note that missing data are treated in the same way as forecasts are handled (see Sections 8.4 and 8.6). In estimating the filtered state, for example, the values of the prediction errors $v_t = y_t - z'_t a_t$ and of the Kalman gains K_t in Kalman filter recursions (8.5) are simply set to zero whenever the value of an observation y_t is missing. This means, of course, that the reverse is also true: forecasts for the unknown future are simply obtained by treating the observations at time points $n + 1$, $n + 2, n + 3, \ldots$ as missing.

9

Multivariate time series analysis*

All state space models discussed in the previous chapters are concerned with the analysis of only one time series. In state space methods such univariate analyses are easily generalised to the situation where two or more (say p) time series need to be analysed simultaneously. This chapter presents an introduction to multivariate state space analysis and discusses some particular issues of interest.

9.1. State space representation of multivariate models

The multivariate time series model can also be represented by the state space form

$$y_t = Z_t a_t + \varepsilon_t, \qquad \varepsilon_t \sim \text{NID}(0, H_t) \qquad (9.1)$$

$$a_{t+1} = T_t a_t + R_t \eta_t \qquad \eta_t \sim \text{NID}(0, Q_t) \qquad (9.2)$$

for $t = 1, \ldots, n$. The observation or measurement equation (9.1) is for a $p \times 1$ vector y_t containing the values of the p observed time series at time point t. The $p \times 1$ irregular vector ε_t contains the p observation disturbances, one for each time series in y_t. The p observation disturbances are assumed to have zero means and an unknown variance–covariance structure represented by a variance matrix H_t of order $p \times p$. The $m \times 1$ state vector a_t contains unobserved variables and unknown fixed effects. Matrix Z_t of order $p \times m$ links the unobservable factors and regression effects of the state vector with the observation vector. Matrix T_t in (9.2) is called the transition matrix of order $m \times m$. The $r \times 1$ vector η_t contains the state disturbances with zero means and unknown variances and covariances collected in the variance matrix Q_t of order $r \times r$. In many standard cases, $r = m$ and matrix R_t is the identity matrix I_m. In other cases, matrix R_t is an $m \times r$ selection matrix with $r < m$. Although matrix R_t can be specified freely, it is often composed of a selection from the r columns of the identity matrix I_m.

9.2. Multivariate trend model with regression effects

To illustrate that the general framework of a state space model can be used for multivariate time series analyses, we consider a case with $p = 2$ and with vectors and matrices given by

$$
\alpha_t = \begin{pmatrix} \mu_t^{(1)} \\ \nu_t^{(1)} \\ \beta_t^{(1)} \\ \mu_t^{(2)} \\ \nu_t^{(2)} \\ \beta_t^{(2)} \end{pmatrix}, \quad
\eta_t = \begin{pmatrix} \xi_t^{(1)} \\ \zeta_t^{(1)} \\ \xi_t^{(2)} \\ \zeta_t^{(2)} \end{pmatrix}, \quad
T_t = \begin{bmatrix}
1 & 1 & 0 & 0 & 0 & 0 \\
0 & 1 & 0 & 0 & 0 & 0 \\
0 & 0 & 1 & 0 & 0 & 0 \\
0 & 0 & 0 & 1 & 1 & 0 \\
0 & 0 & 0 & 0 & 1 & 0 \\
0 & 0 & 0 & 0 & 0 & 1
\end{bmatrix},
$$

$$
R_t = \begin{bmatrix}
1 & 0 & 0 & 0 \\
0 & 1 & 0 & 0 \\
0 & 0 & 0 & 0 \\
0 & 0 & 1 & 0 \\
0 & 0 & 0 & 1 \\
0 & 0 & 0 & 0
\end{bmatrix},
$$

$$
Z_t = \begin{bmatrix}
1 & 0 & x_t & 0 & 0 & 0 \\
0 & 0 & 0 & 1 & 0 & x_t
\end{bmatrix}, \quad
H_t = \begin{bmatrix}
\sigma_{\varepsilon^{(1)}}^2 & \text{cov}(\varepsilon^{(1)}, \varepsilon^{(2)}) \\
\text{cov}(\varepsilon^{(1)}, \varepsilon^{(2)}) & \sigma_{\varepsilon^{(2)}}^2
\end{bmatrix}, \quad \text{and}
$$

$$
Q_t = \begin{bmatrix}
\sigma_{\xi^{(1)}}^2 & 0 & \text{cov}(\xi^{(1)}, \xi^{(2)}) & 0 \\
0 & \sigma_{\zeta^{(1)}}^2 & 0 & \text{cov}(\zeta^{(1)}, \zeta^{(2)}) \\
\text{cov}(\xi^{(1)}, \xi^{(2)}) & 0 & \sigma_{\xi^{(2)}}^2 & 0 \\
0 & \text{cov}(\zeta^{(1)}, \zeta^{(2)}) & 0 & \sigma_{\zeta^{(2)}}^2
\end{bmatrix}.
$$

These matrices imply a bivariate local linear trend model with the same explanatory variable x_t applied to both series in y_t. The superscripts (1) and (2) in the matrices and vectors denote whether they belong to the first or to the second series, respectively. The particular system matrices for matrix equation (9.1) lead to the following two observation equations:

$$y_t^{(1)} = \mu_t^{(1)} + \beta_t^{(1)} x_t + \varepsilon_t^{(1)},$$

$$y_t^{(2)} = \mu_t^{(2)} + \beta_t^{(2)} x_t + \varepsilon_t^{(2)},$$

and those for matrix equation (9.2) result in the following six state equations:

$$\mu_{t+1}^{(1)} = \mu_t^{(1)} + \nu_t^{(1)} + \xi_t^{(1)},$$

$$\nu_{t+1}^{(1)} = \nu_t^{(1)} + \zeta_t^{(1)},$$

$$\beta_{t+1}^{(1)} = \beta_t^{(1)},$$

$$\mu_{t+1}^{(2)} = \mu_t^{(2)} + \nu_t^{(2)} + \xi_t^{(2)},$$

$$\nu_{t+1}^{(2)} = \nu_t^{(2)} + \zeta_t^{(2)},$$

$$\beta_{t+1}^{(2)} = \beta_t^{(2)}.$$

In this example the same model is applied to the two time series under consideration. However, we may also use different state space models for the two series. For example, suppose that we want to include the explanatory variable only in the first equation and not in the second equation. In this case, the vectors and matrices in (9.1) and (9.2) can be set up as:

$$a_t = \begin{pmatrix} \mu_t^{(1)} \\ \nu_t^{(1)} \\ \beta_t^{(1)} \\ \mu_t^{(2)} \\ \nu_t^{(2)} \end{pmatrix}, \quad \eta_t = \begin{pmatrix} \xi_t^{(1)} \\ \zeta_t^{(1)} \\ \xi_t^{(2)} \\ \zeta_t^{(2)} \end{pmatrix}, \quad T_t = \begin{bmatrix} 1 & 1 & 0 & 0 & 0 \\ 0 & 1 & 0 & 0 & 0 \\ 0 & 0 & 1 & 0 & 0 \\ 0 & 0 & 0 & 1 & 1 \\ 0 & 0 & 0 & 0 & 1 \end{bmatrix}, \quad R_t = \begin{bmatrix} 1 & 0 & 0 & 0 \\ 0 & 1 & 0 & 0 \\ 0 & 0 & 0 & 0 \\ 0 & 0 & 1 & 0 \\ 0 & 0 & 0 & 1 \end{bmatrix},$$

$$Z_t = \begin{bmatrix} 1 & 0 & x_t & 0 & 0 \\ 0 & 0 & 0 & 1 & 0 \end{bmatrix}, \quad H_t = \begin{bmatrix} \sigma_{\varepsilon^{(1)}}^2 & \text{cov}(\varepsilon^{(1)}, \varepsilon^{(2)}) \\ \text{cov}(\varepsilon^{(1)}, \varepsilon^{(2)}) & \sigma_{\varepsilon^{(2)}}^2 \end{bmatrix}, \quad \text{and}$$

$$Q_t = \begin{bmatrix} \sigma_{\xi^{(1)}}^2 & 0 & \text{cov}(\xi^{(1)}, \xi^{(2)}) & 0 \\ 0 & \sigma_{\zeta^{(1)}}^2 & 0 & \text{cov}(\zeta^{(1)}, \zeta^{(2)}) \\ \text{cov}(\xi^{(1)}, \xi^{(2)}) & 0 & \sigma_{\xi^{(2)}}^2 & 0 \\ 0 & \text{cov}(\zeta^{(1)}, \zeta^{(2)}) & 0 & \sigma_{\zeta^{(2)}}^2 \end{bmatrix}.$$

We then obtain the observation equations

$$y_t^{(1)} = \mu_t^{(1)} + \beta_t^{(1)} x_t + \varepsilon_t^{(1)},$$

$$y_t^{(2)} = \mu_t^{(2)} + \varepsilon_t^{(2)},$$

and the five state equations

$$\mu_{t+1}^{(1)} = \mu_t^{(1)} + v_t^{(1)} + \xi_t^{(1)},$$

$$v_{t+1}^{(1)} = v_t^{(1)} + \zeta_t^{(1)},$$

$$\beta_{t+1}^{(1)} = \beta_t^{(1)},$$

$$\mu_{t+1}^{(2)} = \mu_t^{(2)} + v_t^{(2)} + \xi_t^{(2)},$$

$$v_{t+1}^{(2)} = v_t^{(2)} + \zeta_t^{(2)}.$$

In some cases it may be convenient to have matrix Q_t as a block diagonal matrix. After some permutations of rows and columns of the vectors and matrices, matrix Q_t can be represented as a block diagonal matrix without any alteration to the underlying model. For example, in this case the state space vectors and matrices are

$$a_t = \begin{pmatrix} \mu_t^{(1)} \\ \mu_t^{(2)} \\ v_t^{(1)} \\ v_t^{(2)} \\ \beta_t^{(1)} \end{pmatrix}, \quad \eta_t = \begin{pmatrix} \xi_t^{(1)} \\ \xi_t^{(2)} \\ \zeta_t^{(1)} \\ \zeta_t^{(2)} \end{pmatrix}, \quad T_t = \begin{bmatrix} 1 & 0 & 1 & 0 & 0 \\ 0 & 1 & 0 & 1 & 0 \\ 0 & 0 & 1 & 0 & 0 \\ 0 & 0 & 0 & 1 & 0 \\ 0 & 0 & 0 & 0 & 1 \end{bmatrix}, \quad R_t = \begin{bmatrix} 1 & 0 & 0 & 0 \\ 0 & 1 & 0 & 0 \\ 0 & 0 & 1 & 0 \\ 0 & 0 & 0 & 1 \\ 0 & 0 & 0 & 0 \end{bmatrix},$$

$$Z_t = \begin{bmatrix} 1 & 0 & 0 & 0 & x_t \\ 0 & 1 & 0 & 0 & 0 \end{bmatrix}, \quad H_t = \begin{bmatrix} \sigma_{\varepsilon^{(1)}}^2 & \text{cov}(\varepsilon^{(1)}, \varepsilon^{(2)}) \\ \text{cov}(\varepsilon^{(1)}, \varepsilon^{(2)}) & \sigma_{\varepsilon^{(2)}}^2 \end{bmatrix}, \quad \text{and}$$

$$Q_t = \begin{bmatrix} \sigma_{\xi^{(1)}}^2 & \text{cov}(\xi^{(1)}, \xi^{(2)}) & 0 & 0 \\ \text{cov}(\xi^{(1)}, \xi^{(2)}) & \sigma_{\xi^{(2)}}^2 & 0 & 0 \\ 0 & 0 & \sigma_{\zeta^{(1)}}^2 & \text{cov}(\zeta^{(1)}, \zeta^{(2)}) \\ 0 & 0 & \text{cov}(\zeta^{(1)}, \zeta^{(2)}) & \sigma_{\zeta^{(2)}}^2 \end{bmatrix},$$

leading to

$$y_t^{(1)} = \mu_t^{(1)} + \beta_t^{(1)} x_t + \varepsilon_t^{(1)},$$

$$y_t^{(2)} = \mu_t^{(2)} + \varepsilon_t^{(2)},$$

for the observation equations and

$$\mu_{t+1}^{(1)} = \mu_t^{(1)} + v_t^{(1)} + \xi_t^{(1)},$$

$$\mu_{t+1}^{(2)} = \mu_t^{(2)} + v_t^{(2)} + \xi_t^{(2)},$$

$$v_{t+1}^{(1)} = v_t^{(1)} + \zeta_t^{(1)},$$

$$v_{t+1}^{(2)} = v_t^{(2)} + \zeta_t^{(2)},$$

$$\beta_{t+1}^{(1)} = \beta_t^{(1)},$$

for the five state equations. Apart from the fact that the order of appearance in the state vector has changed, the equations of the underlying model remain completely identical.

9.3. Common levels and slopes

In a multivariate state space analysis, the observation and state equations have disturbances associated with a particular component or irregular. In the examples of the previous sections, the disturbances $\zeta_t^{(1)}$ and $\zeta_t^{(2)}$ are associated with the slope components $v_t^{(1)}$ and $v_t^{(2)}$, respectively. When the disturbances are uncorrelated, that is $\text{cov}(\zeta^{(1)}, \zeta^{(2)}) = 0$, the slope components are independent. The slope components become related to each other when the slope disturbances are correlated, that is, when $\text{cov}(\zeta^{(1)}, \zeta^{(2)}) \neq 0$. The multivariate time series model with unobserved component vectors that depend on correlated disturbances is referred to as a *seemingly unrelated time series equations* model. The name underlines the fact that although the disturbances of the components can be correlated, the equations remain 'seemingly unrelated'.

The level of dependence is measured most effectively by the correlation between the two disturbances as given by

$$\text{corr}(\zeta^{(1)}, \zeta^{(2)}) = \frac{\text{cov}(\zeta^{(1)}, \zeta^{(2)})}{\sqrt{\sigma_{\zeta^{(1)}}^2 \sigma_{\zeta^{(2)}}^2}},$$

where $-1 \leq \text{corr}(\zeta^{(1)}, \zeta^{(2)}) \leq 1$. When the correlation is close to zero, the slope components do not have much in common. The slopes have much in common when the correlation is close to plus or minus one. In the extreme case of $\text{corr}(\zeta^{(1)}, \zeta^{(2)}) = \pm 1$, a particular slope component, say $v_t^{(2)}$, can be expressed as a linear combination of the other slope, say $v_t^{(1)}$. In particular, we have $v_t^{(2)} = a + b v_t^{(1)}$ when the slope disturbances are perfectly

correlated. In this case, slope components are said to be *common*. In the
case of $-1 < \text{corr}(\zeta^{(1)}, \zeta^{(2)}) < 1$, the variance matrix

$$\begin{bmatrix} \sigma^2_{\zeta^{(1)}} & \text{cov}(\zeta^{(1)}, \zeta^{(2)}) \\ \text{cov}(\zeta^{(1)}, \zeta^{(2)}) & \sigma^2_{\zeta^{(2)}} \end{bmatrix},$$

has rank two. In the case of $\text{corr}(\zeta^{(1)}, \zeta^{(2)}) = \pm 1$, the rank of this variance
matrix equals 1.

It follows that the rank of the variance matrix determines whether components are common. For multivariate models with $p > 2$ and a variance
matrix with rank $q > 0$, the number of common components is equal
to q and the number of rank restrictions is $r = p - q$. This framework is
closely related to factor analysis and principal component analysis. When
$r = p - q$ rank restrictions are exercised, the p slope components are the
result of linear combinations of q common slope components. In the
literature, a multivariate state space model is therefore sometimes also
referred to as a *dynamic factor analysis model*.

The same arguments apply to the disturbances of other components
and the irregular vector ϵ_t. For example, when the variance matrix of the
disturbance vector associated with the level component, that is

$$\begin{bmatrix} \sigma^2_{\xi^{(1)}} & \text{cov}(\xi^{(1)}, \xi^{(2)}) \\ \text{cov}(\xi^{(1)}, \xi^{(2)}) & \sigma^2_{\xi^{(2)}} \end{bmatrix},$$

has rank one, we have $\text{corr}(\xi^{(1)}, \xi^{(2)}) = \pm 1$. In the case of a bivariate local
level model (this is the trend model of the previous section but without
a slope component and a regression effect), the level component is said
to be common. The two level components in the model can be expressed
as linear combinations of each other. However, for a level component
with a stochastic bivariate slope component that has a full rank variance
matrix for $\zeta_t^{(1)}$ and $\zeta_t^{(2)}$ and with disturbances $\xi_t^{(1)}$ and $\xi_t^{(2)}$ that are fully
correlated, the resulting level component is not common. Due to the
slope component, the level components cannot be expressed as linear
functions of each other. Such issues are important in practice for a correct
interpretation of the results in a multivariate time series analysis.

Generally, a variance matrix is unknown and needs to be estimated.
The estimated coefficients determine the rank of the matrix and therefore
the nature of the relationship between the individual elements of the
component vector. In particular cases, it may be necessary or interesting
to enforce rank restrictions. The rank of a particular variance matrix can
be imposed by considering the decomposition of a symmetric positive

semi-definite matrix such as

$$
\begin{bmatrix}
\sigma^2_{\zeta^{(1)}} & \mathrm{cov}(\zeta^{(1)}, \zeta^{(2)}) \\
\mathrm{cov}(\zeta^{(1)}, \zeta^{(2)}) & \sigma^2_{\zeta^{(2)}}
\end{bmatrix}
=
\begin{bmatrix}
a & 0 \\
b & c
\end{bmatrix}
\begin{bmatrix}
a & b \\
0 & c
\end{bmatrix},
$$

with coefficients $a, c \geq 0$. The lower triangular structure of the right-hand side matrices is chosen to have the same number of coefficients as in the variance matrix of the left-hand side and to enforce a positive semi-definite variance matrix. By restricting $c = 0$ and estimating the remaining b and c, the resulting estimated variance matrix is clearly always of rank one.

The issue of common levels and slopes is important since it is often of interest to find the common behaviour between the different time series in a multivariate time series analysis. The existence of a common component can lead to more insights in certain aspects of the time series of interest. An illustration of this is given in the next section.

Finally, if the variance matrices H_t and Q_t in (9.1) and (9.2) are restricted to be *diagonal* (and the rows of Z_t are orthogonal, and T_t is appropriately chosen), we actually carry out p separate univariate analyses. In this case we should label the model as a 'really unrelated' time series equations model. For further details and extensions of multivariate time series analysis, we refer to Harvey (1989).

9.4. An illustration of multivariate state space analysis

This section addresses the practical implications of a multivariate state space analysis. Various results of a simultaneous analysis of two time series will be discussed in some detail. The first series consists of the log of the monthly numbers of *front* seat passengers killed or seriously injured in the UK for the period 1969–1984. The second series consists of the log of the monthly numbers of *rear* seat passengers killed or seriously injured (KSI) in the UK during the same period. The graphs of these two series are shown in Figure 9.1. Appendix C contains the actual numbers from these two series (not their logs).

Two explanatory variables and one intervention variable are added to the local level model with a seasonal component for both series. The explanatory variables are the log of the petrol price (as given in Appendix A), and the log of the number of kilometres travelled (as given in Appendix C). The intervention variable is the introduction of the seat belt law in February 1983.

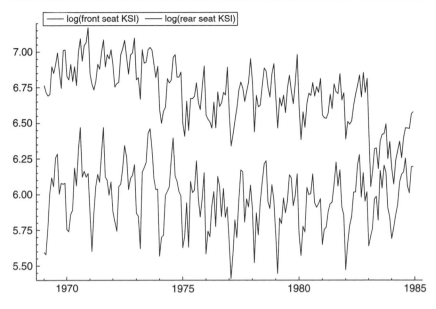

Figure 9.1. Log of monthly numbers of front seat passengers (top) and rear seat passengers (bottom) killed or seriously injured in the UK in the period 1969–1984.

The bivariate time series analysis aims to assess the effect of the introduction of the seat belt law in a more convincing setting than was done in Sections 7.3 and 8.6. The intervention is expected to affect the front seat car passengers and not the rear seat car passengers. Therefore, the former series can be considered as a *treatment* series while the latter series can be used as a *control* series. If we can show that the treatment series was significantly affected by the seat belt law, while the control series was not, we have an even stronger case in favour of the effect of this law than before.

The multivariate analysis of the two series starts with considering the local level model with seasonal of Chapter 4 but applied to both series simultaneously. Subsequently, the intervention variable for the introduction of the law in February 1983 and the explanatory variables (petrol price and number of kilometres travelled, both in logs) are included in the two equations of the bivariate model. Since the variances for the seasonal components of the treatment and control series are both found to be almost equal to zero, this component is treated deterministically in both series. Unrestricted estimation of the level variance matrix of the treatment and control series yields the following results. The estimate of

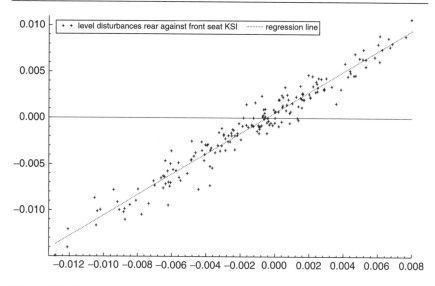

Figure 9.2. Level disturbances for rear seat (horizontal) versus front seat KSI (vertical) in a seemingly unrelated model.

the variance matrix of the two irregular components for this bivariate state space model equals

$$H = \begin{bmatrix} 0.0054281 & 0.0044834 \\ 0.0044834 & 0.0085138 \end{bmatrix},$$

while the estimate of the variance matrix of the level disturbances corresponding to the front and rear seat passengers KSI is

$$Q = \begin{bmatrix} 0.00025881 & 0.00022546 \\ 0.00022546 & 0.00023227 \end{bmatrix}.$$

Figure 9.2 contains a scatter plot of the level disturbances obtained with this analysis, together with the best fitting regression line. It shows the strong positive linear relationship between the level disturbances of the treatment and the control series. Their correlation is, in fact, 0.9743. This means that the two levels themselves, which are displayed in Figure 9.3, must also be highly correlated.

This is confirmed by the scatter plot of the two level components (see Figure 9.4), together with the best fitting regression line. As Figures 9.3 and 9.4 indicate, the two level components have a tendency to increase and decrease at the same points in time.

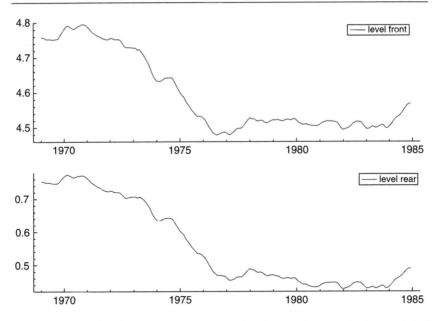

Figure 9.3. Levels of treatment and control series in the seemingly unrelated model.

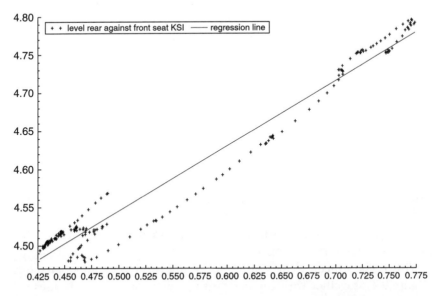

Figure 9.4. Level of treatment against level of control series in the seemingly unrelated model.

The estimated regression coefficient for the intervention variable is -0.3372 in the treatment series and 0.0021 in the control series. The t-tests indicate that the intervention coefficient for the treatment series is highly significant while it is not significant for the control series. The analysis is therefore repeated but with two important modifications. First, the intervention variable is removed from the model for rear seat passengers KSI (the control series). Second, the *rank* of the corresponding variance matrix is restricted to *one* since the level disturbances of the two series are highly correlated in the first analysis. The implications of a rank reduction are discussed in the previous section. The number of parameters in the second model is reduced by two (i.e. one for the intervention in the control series, and one for the variance matrix of the level disturbances). We therefore have a more parsimonious description of the data.

The estimate of the variance matrix of the irregular components for this second bivariate state space model equals

$$H = \begin{bmatrix} 0.0054747 & 0.0044166 \\ 0.0044166 & 0.0088022 \end{bmatrix},$$

while the estimate of the variance matrix of the level disturbances is

$$Q = \begin{bmatrix} 0.00023264 & 0.00022096 \\ 0.00022096 & 0.00020986 \end{bmatrix}.$$

The rank of the latter variance matrix is indeed one, because the second eigenvalue in the eigenvalue decomposition of the matrix is zero. Specifically, this variance matrix can be written as

$$Q = \begin{bmatrix} 0.01525259 \\ 0.01448661 \end{bmatrix} \begin{bmatrix} 0.01525259 & 0.01448661 \end{bmatrix},$$

meaning that the level disturbances of the treatment and control series are now *proportional* to one another. This property is illustrated graphically in Figure 9.5, which contains a scatter plot of these two level disturbances.

The level disturbance of the treatment series can be perfectly predicted from those of the control series with the regression equation

$$\xi_t^{(1)} = 1.0529\, \xi_t^{(2)}$$

for $t = 1, \ldots, n$. This automatically implies that the levels of the two series must also be perfectly linearly related (see Figure 9.6). The regression equation for the two level components in Figure 9.6 is

$$\mu_t^{(1)} = 2.3115 + 1.0529\, \mu_t^{(2)},$$

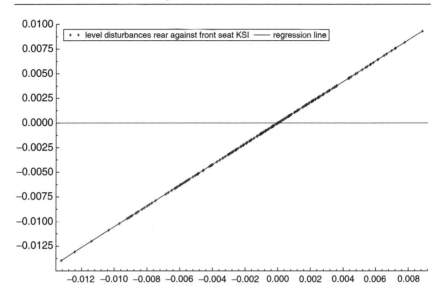

Figure 9.5. Level disturbances for rear (horizontal) against front seat KSI (vertical), rank one model.

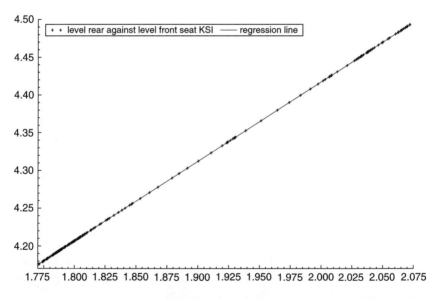

Figure 9.6. Level of treatment against level of control series in rank one model.

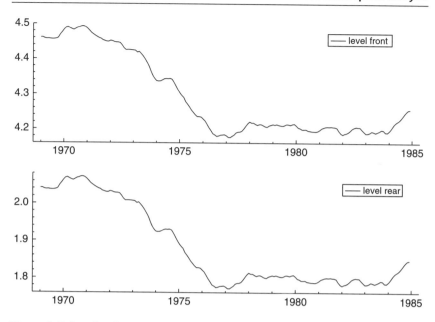

Figure 9.7. Levels of treatment and control series, rank one model.

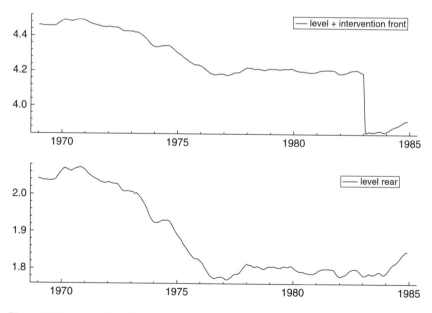

Figure 9.8. Level of treatment series plus intervention, and level of control series, rank one model.

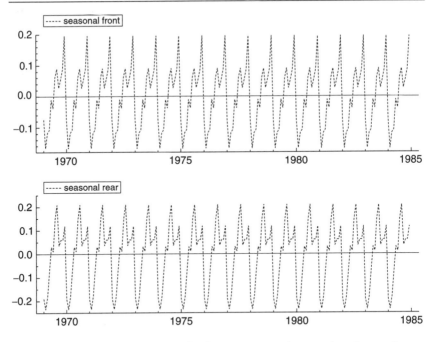

Figure 9.9. Deterministic seasonal of treatment and control series, rank one model.

for $t = 1, \ldots, n$. The perfect linear relationship between the two stochastic levels is also confirmed by inspecting their graphs in Figure 9.7: they are identical up to an overall difference in level (which is equal to 2.3115) and in rate of change (which is equal to 1.0529).

The estimated value of the regression weight for the intervention variable applied to the treatment series only is −0.3387, and the result of adding this state component to the level of the treatment series is shown in Figure 9.8 (compared to Figure 9.7 the level of the control series is unchanged since no intervention was modelled for this series). To complete the output of the analysis, graphs of the estimated deterministic seasonal components of the treatment and control series in the restricted bivariate analysis are presented in Figure 9.9.

An interesting by-product of the second analysis is the considerable increase in the value of the t-test for the intervention coefficient of the treatment series. The value of this t-test in the second analysis is more than two and a half times larger than the one in the first analysis.

While the t-value for the intervention parameter is -6.8167 in the first analysis, it is -17.2852 in the second analysis. Since the intervention coefficients themselves are quite similar in the two analyses (i.e. -0.3372 and -0.3387 in the first and second analyses, respectively), the most important reason for the increase in the value of the t-test is the large decrease in the sum of squared one-step ahead prediction errors.

10

State space and Box–Jenkins methods for time series analysis

Box–Jenkins methods for time series analysis are popular and widely applied. The purpose of this chapter is to provide a short introduction to these methods and to discuss the relative merits of state space and Box–Jenkins methods. For a more in-depth exposition of Box–Jenkins time series analysis, we refer to the very accessible book by Chatfield (2004), and to the mathematically advanced classic book by Box and Jenkins (1976). The Box–Jenkins approach is based on autoregressive integrated moving average (ARIMA) models. To provide some discussion of the different approaches of time series, we need to introduce concepts related to stationary time series, autoregressive processes, moving average processes and differencing. Further it is shown how these concepts are used in the Box–Jenkins approach to time series analysis. Finally, the relation with unobserved components is hinted at and a short discussion on the differences between both approaches is presented.

10.1. Stationary processes and related concepts

Short definitions of stochastic processes involved in the modelling of times series with the Box–Jenkins approach are covered in the following sections.

10.1.1. *Stationary process*

A stochastic process μ_t is called a *second-order stationary* (or *weakly stationary*) process if its mean, variance and autocovariances are constant over time. The autocovariances vary with the corresponding lag periods. Similarly to autocorrelations (see Chapter 1), autocovariances are the covariances between a series μ_t and the same series shifted k time points into the future. The stationary property states that the covariances between μ_t and μ_{t+k} are the same, irrespective of index t, but may be different for different k. Note that the covariance becomes a variance when $k = 0$. Examples of realisations of weakly stationary processes can be found in Figures 10.1, 10.5, 10.7 and 10.9 below. In contrast, Figure 10.3 contains a typical example of the realisation of a non-stationary process, since the mean of this series continuously changes over time.

10.1.2. Random process

A stochastic process is called a *purely random* process if it consists of random variables η_t which are mutually independent and identically distributed. Since this implies that the process has constant mean and variance, a purely random process is always a stationary process. Moreover, for all $k \neq t$ the autocorrelations between η_t and η_{t+k} of a purely random process are zero. Figure 10.1 contains an example of the realisation of a random process obtained by drawing a random sample of $N = 200$ observations from a normal distribution. The residual plots displayed in Figures 2.6, 3.6, 4.9, and 7.4 for stochastic state space models may also be considered as examples of realisations of a random process.

An important diagnostic tool for unravelling the possible theoretical processes underlying an observed time series is the correlogram, as discussed in Chapter 1. The correlogram for the first 12 lags of the data shown in Figure 10.1 is given in Figure 10.2. As noted before, the independence of the variables η_t of a random process is reflected in the fact that all autocorrelation coefficients are approximately equal to zero.

Let η_t be a purely random process. Then a process μ_t is called a *random walk* if

$$\mu_{t+1} = \mu_1 + \sum_{j=1}^{t} \eta_j = \mu_t + \eta_t, \tag{10.1}$$

for some unknown value of μ_1. Many state components in the models presented in Chapters 2–7 are random walks or variations of it. It follows from (10.1) that the first differences of a random walk equal

$$\Delta \mu_t = \mu_t - \mu_{t-1} = \eta_{t-1}.$$

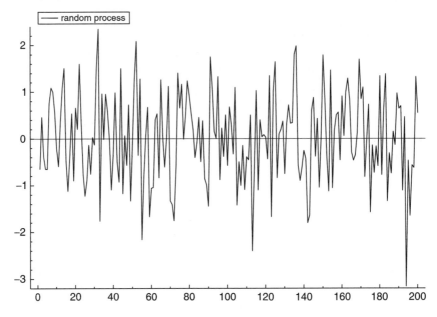

Figure 10.1. Realisation of a random process.

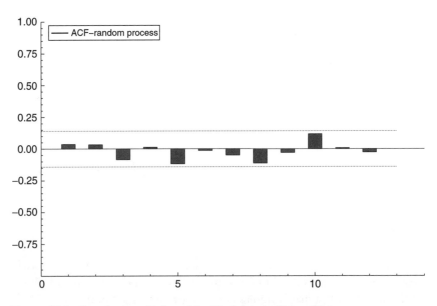

Figure 10.2. Correlogram for lags 1 to 12 of data in Figure 10.1.

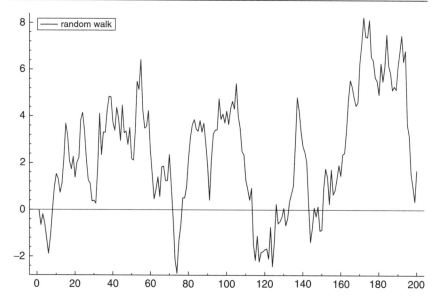

Figure 10.3. Example of a random walk with $\mu_1 = 0$.

The first differences of a random walk yield a stationary random process. If we compute the values of μ_t with (10.1) using the values for η_t shown in Figure 10.1, and start with $\mu_1 = 0$, we obtain the time series displayed in Figure 10.3. As Figure 10.3 clearly indicates, a random walk is a nonstationary process because the mean of the series changes over time. Figure 10.4 displays the correlogram of the data in Figure 10.3. The pattern of autocorrelations displayed in Figure 10.4 is typical for non-stationary processes: the values of the autocorrelations only start approaching zero for very large values of the lag.

10.1.3. *Moving average process*

Let η_t be a purely random process with mean zero and variance σ^2. Then a process μ_t is called a moving average process of order q (abbreviated as an MA(q) process) if

$$\mu_t = \beta_0 \eta_t + \beta_1 \eta_{t-1} + \beta_2 \eta_{t-2} + \cdots + \beta_q \eta_{t-q}. \tag{10.2}$$

An example of a first-order MA(1) process is given by

$$\mu_t = \eta_t + 0.5 \eta_{t-1}.$$

125

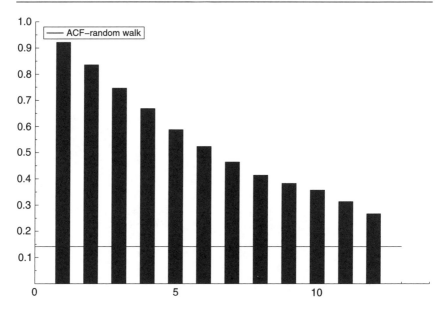

Figure 10.4. Correlogram for lags 1 to 12 of the data in Figure 10.3.

If we compute the values of μ_t with the latter formula using the values for η_t shown in Figure 10.1, we obtain the time series displayed in Figure 10.5. The correlogram for the series in Figure 10.5 is given in Figure 10.6.

In case $\beta_0 = 1$ in (10.2), the first order autocorrelation of a pure MA(1) process equals

$$\frac{\beta_1}{1 + \beta_1^2} = \frac{0.5}{1 + 0.5^2} = 0.4,$$

as can be verified in the correlogram in Figure 10.6. Moreover, the first q autocorrelations of a pure MA(q) process typically deviate from zero, while they are zero for lags $j > q$. A pure MA(q) process is always a stationary process.

10.1.4. *Autoregressive process*

Let η_t be a purely random process with mean zero and variance σ^2. Then a process μ_t is called an autoregressive process of order p (abbreviated as an AR(p) process) if

$$\mu_t = a_1 \mu_{t-1} + a_2 \mu_{t-2} + \cdots + a_p \mu_{t-p} + \eta_t. \tag{10.3}$$

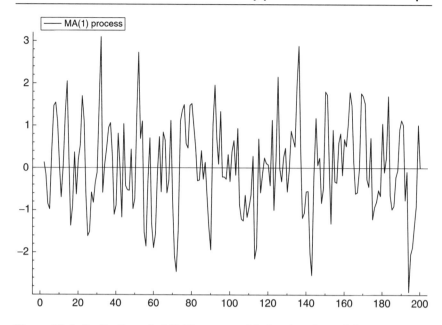

Figure 10.5. Realisation of a MA(1) process with $\beta_0 = 1$ and $\beta_1 = 0.5$.

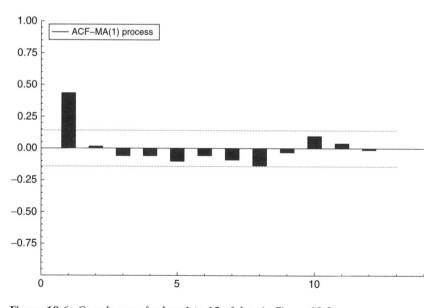

Figure 10.6. Correlogram for lags 1 to 12 of data in Figure 10.5.

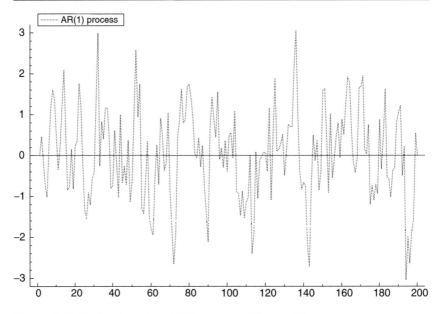

Figure 10.7. Realisation of an AR(1) process with $a_1 = 0.5$.

In this case, μ_t is regressed on past values of itself. For example, if we compute the values of μ_t according to the first-order AR(1) process

$$\mu_t = 0.5\,\mu_{t-1} + \eta_t,$$

and use the values for η_t shown in Figure 10.1, we obtain the time series displayed in Figure 10.7.

The first autocorrelation of a pure AR(1) process can be proven to be equal to a_1 in (10.3). For the AR(1) process in Figure 10.7, the first autocorrelation is therefore $a_1 = 0.5$, as can be verified to be approximately true in the correlogram in Figure 10.8. The higher autocorrelations for the AR(1) process are given by a_1^k where k is the corresponding lag. A pure AR(p) process is a stationary process when the coefficients are within the unit circle. For the AR(1) process, it implies that $|a_1| < 1$.

10.1.5. Autoregressive moving average process

By combining moving average (10.2) and autoregressive (10.3) processes, what is known as the autoregressive moving average (ARMA) model is obtained. An ARMA model with p AR terms and q MA terms is called an

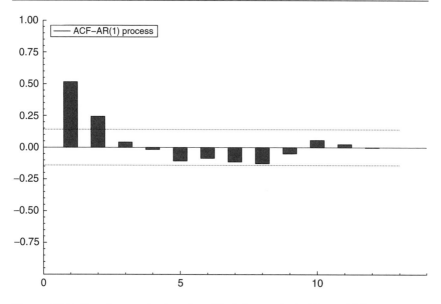

Figure 10.8. Correlogram for lags 1 to 12 of time series in Figure 10.7.

ARMA(p, q) process, and is written as

$$\mu_t = a_1 \mu_{t-1} + a_2 \mu_{t-2} + \cdots + a_p \mu_{t-p} + \eta_t + \beta_1 \eta_{t-1}$$

$$+ \beta_2 \eta_{t-2} + \cdots + \beta_q \eta_{t-q}, \qquad (10.4)$$

where the variables η_t are a random process. For example, if we compute the values of μ_t according to the ARMA(1, 1) process

$$\mu_t = 0.5 \mu_{t-1} + \eta_t + 0.5 \eta_{t-1},$$

and use the values for η_t shown in Figure 10.1, we obtain the stationary process shown in Figure 10.9. Figure 10.10 contains the correlogram for the series in Figure 10.9.

10.2. Non-stationary ARIMA models

A typical Box–Jenkins approach to time series analysis proceeds along the following lines. In practice, some non-stationary features in the time series are present due to trend and/or seasonal effects. As a first step, the observed time series is transformed into a stationary series using time and lag functions. In practice, the trend and/or seasonal are removed from the

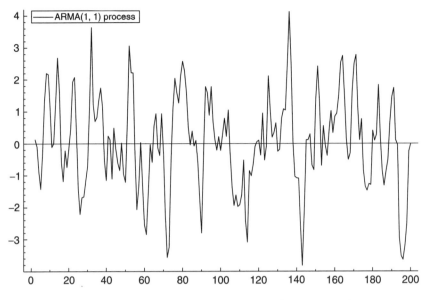

Figure 10.9. Realisation of an ARMA(1, 1) process with $\alpha_1 = \beta_1 = 0.5$.

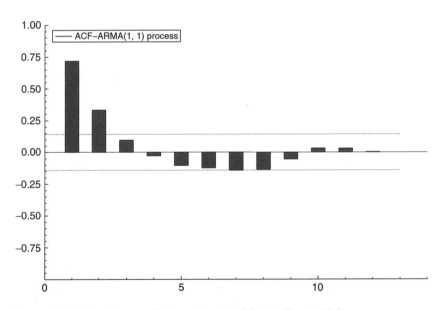

Figure 10.10. Correlogram for lags 1 to 12 of data in Figure 10.9.

series by *differencing*. A non-stationary random walk μ_t can be turned into a random (stationary) process by taking the first differences since

$$\Delta \mu_t = \mu_t - \mu_{t-1} = \eta_{t-1}.$$

Similarly, letting y_t denote an observed time series, differencing involves the computation of a new variable y_t^* satisfying

$$y_t^* = \Delta y_t = y_t - y_{t-1},$$

to remove the trend in the series, and

$$y_t^* = \Delta_s y_t = y_t - y_{t-s},$$

to remove a seasonal with periodicity s from the series. In some cases a combined removal of trend and seasonal is necessary and is achieved by

$$y_t^* = \Delta \Delta_s y_t = (y_t - y_{t-s}) - (y_{t-1} - y_{t-s-1}).$$

In cases y_t^* is still not stationary, the differencing procedure can be continued by taking second differences

$$y_t^* = \Delta^2 \Delta_s^2 y_t,$$

or even third differences. This process of differencing an observed time series in order to obtain an approximate stationary series is referred to as *integration*. After sufficient differencing is applied to obtain an approximate stationary time series, the appropriate AR(p), MA(q) or ARMA(p, q) models need to be identified that can best account for the differenced observed time series.

For example, suppose that the transformed time series of interest is the series displayed in Figure 10.9. The task of the researcher is to determine the correct ARMA(1, 1) model. The optimal parameter estimates of the model are $a_1 = \beta_1 = 0.5$. Of course, once the correct model is identified, the residuals η_t in equation (10.4) should satisfy the properties of a random process, and therefore should result in a correlogram similar to the one displayed in Figure 10.2.

Summarising, ARIMA models are fitted using the following steps:

1. Non-stationary features due to trend and seasonal effects are removed from the observed time series by differencing. The resulting time series should be (more or less) stationary.

2. The actual analysis is performed by fitting an ARMA(p, q) model on the transformed time series. The residuals of the best fitting ARMA(p, q) model should follow a random process.

ARIMA models are usually written as ARIMA(p, d, q) where

   p is the order of the autoregressive component,
   q is the order of the moving average component, and
   d is the number of differences taken prior to the actual analysis.

For example, if an observed time series is generated by a random walk process, the ARIMA(0, 1, 0) model should provide the best representation of the series. Taking first differences yields a series that is both stationary and random. No further analysis is required in this case.

10.3. Unobserved components and ARIMA

There are a number of important similarities between state space and ARIMA models. For instance, the local level model (see Chapter 2) is given by

$$y_t = \mu_t + \varepsilon_t, \tag{10.5}$$

$$\mu_t = \mu_{t-1} + \eta_t. \tag{10.6}$$

The first differences of y_t are equal to

$$\Delta y_t = y_t - y_{t-1} = \mu_t - \mu_{t-1} + \varepsilon_t - \varepsilon_{t-1}. \tag{10.7}$$

It follows from (10.6) that

$$\mu_t - \mu_{t-1} = \eta_t, \tag{10.8}$$

and substitution of (10.8) in (10.7) yields

$$\Delta y_t = y_t - y_{t-1} = \eta_t + \varepsilon_t - \varepsilon_{t-1}. \tag{10.9}$$

It can be shown that (10.9) is a stationary process which has the same correlogram as the MA(1) process. This implies that the local level model is equivalent to an ARIMA(0, 1, 1) model.

For a second example of the similarity between state space and ARIMA modelling, we consider the local linear trend model (see Chapter 3) as given by

$$y_t = \mu_t + \varepsilon_t, \tag{10.10}$$

$$\mu_t = \mu_{t-1} + v_{t-1} + \xi_{t-1}, \tag{10.11}$$

$$v_t = v_{t-1} + \zeta_{t-1}. \tag{10.12}$$

Taking first differences of y_t in (10.10) yields

$$\Delta y_t = y_t - y_{t-1} = \mu_t - \mu_{t-1} + \varepsilon_t - \varepsilon_{t-1}, \tag{10.13}$$

and the second differences are therefore equal to

$$\Delta^2 y_t = y_t - y_{t-1} - (y_{t-1} - y_{t-2}) = y_t - 2 y_{t-1} + y_{t-2}$$

$$= \mu_t + \varepsilon_t - 2(\mu_{t-1} + \varepsilon_{t-1}) + (\mu_{t-2} + \varepsilon_{t-2})$$

$$= (\mu_t - \mu_{t-1}) - (\mu_{t-1} - \mu_{t-2}) + \varepsilon_t - 2\varepsilon_{t-1} + \varepsilon_{t-2}. \tag{10.14}$$

It follows from (10.11) that

$$\mu_t - \mu_{t-1} = v_{t-1} + \xi_{t-1}, \tag{10.15}$$

and

$$\mu_{t-1} - \mu_{t-2} = v_{t-2} + \xi_{t-2}. \tag{10.16}$$

Substitution of (10.15) and (10.16) in (10.14) yields

$$\Delta^2 y_t = (v_{t-1} + \xi_{t-1}) - (v_{t-2} + \xi_{t-2}) + \varepsilon_t - 2\varepsilon_{t-1} + \varepsilon_{t-2}$$

$$= (v_{t-1} - v_{t-2}) + \xi_{t-1} - \xi_{t-2} + \varepsilon_t - 2\varepsilon_{t-1} + \varepsilon_{t-2}. \tag{10.17}$$

Finally, it follows from (10.12) that

$$v_{t-1} - v_{t-2} = \zeta_{t-2}, \tag{10.18}$$

and substitution of (10.18) in (10.17) yields

$$\Delta^2 y_t = \zeta_{t-2} + \xi_{t-1} - \xi_{t-2} + \varepsilon_t - 2\varepsilon_{t-1} + \varepsilon_{t-2}. \tag{10.19}$$

It can be shown that (10.19) is a stationary process yielding the same correlogram as a MA(2) model. The local linear trend model is therefore equivalent to an ARIMA(0, 2, 2) model. For a comprehensive overview of these equivalencies between state space and ARIMA models, we refer to Appendix 1 in Harvey (1989). Finally, it should be noted that ARIMA models can also be put in state space form and fitted by state space methods too.

10.4. State space versus ARIMA approaches

Despite the relationships between ARIMA and unobserved components time series models, the Box–Jenkins and state space approaches to time series analysis are distinct. Chapters 2, 3, and 4 present explicit descriptions of non-stationary time series in terms of trend and seasonal components. Such components are explicitly modelled in the state space approach. In the Box–Jenkins approach, trend and seasonal effects are treated as nuisance parameters. These effects are removed from the series before any analysis can begin. As a result, state space methods provide an explicit structural framework for the decomposition of time series in order to diagnose all the dynamics in the time series data simultaneously. Box–Jenkins methods are concerned with the short-term dynamics only and are therefore primarily concerned with forecasting only.

A successful application of ARIMA models requires the (differenced) time series to be stationary. However, as Durbin and Koopman (2001, p. 53) pointed out: 'In the economic and social fields, real series are never stationary however much differencing is done. The investigator has to face the question, how close to stationary is close enough? This is a hard question to answer.' In state space methods, stationarity of the time series is not required. Furthermore, missing data, time-varying regression coefficients and multivariate extensions are easily handled in the state space framework. This handling is relatively difficult in a pure ARIMA modelling context.

11

State space modelling in practice

In this chapter we discuss how to perform a time series analysis based on models discussed in Chapters 1–9 and by using software tools. In particular, we shall consider two time series packages. The first is the user-friendly software package STAMP of Koopman et al. (2000). The second software package is SsfPack of Koopman et al. (1999).

STAMP is an easy-to-use package designed to model and forecast time series, based on structural time series models. The program uses advanced techniques, such as Kalman filtering, but is set up so as to be easy to use. The required basic level that is required is presented in the earlier Chapters 1–9. The hard work is done by the STAMP program, leaving the user free to concentrate on formulating models and analysing time series. In many cases the ultimate aim is then to use the models to make forecasts.

SsfPack is a set of C routines collected in a library that can be linked to the Ox matrix programming language of Doornik (2001). Another link that is established is with S-PLUS, see Zivot and Wang (2003). The analyses presented in this book have been carried out by SsfPack using the link with Ox Professional. All figures in the book are generated by the Ox Professional package. In the following sections, we assume that you are familiar with the Ox programming language. If you are not, please consult the introductory treatment by Doornik and Ooms (2002) or the comprehensive documentation on Doornik's website www.doornik.com.

11.1. The STAMP program and SsfPack

STAMP is the acronym for structural time series analyser, modeller and predictor. It started as a software program for the MS-DOS operating system and since 2000 it has been available for the MS Windows system.

The software operates within the OxMetrics family of econometric and statistical software products. For example, STAMP works with the GiveWin program that enables the handling of data, produces graphical and text output, etc. Nowadays, the program is multi-platform and can be used, for example, on both Windows and Linux platforms.

All models that are discussed in this book except for the models used in the Box–Jenkins approach of time series analysis, can be treated by the STAMP program. This includes both univariate and multivariate models. Although the results in this book are generated by the Ox/SsfPack software (see next sections), most results are verified with STAMP. All results have been similar apart from some numerical differences.

SsfPack is a library of C functions for state space methods. The functions can be linked to C programs in a standard way. However, a link is also established for the object-oriented matrix programming language Ox of Doornik (2001). This link is user-friendly so that state space computations can be implemented in a fast way. This link is documented in Koopman et al. (1999) and details of installation can be found at www.ssfpack.com. In the remainder of this chapter we present an introduction to how SsfPack can be used. Further, some details are given about how parameters are estimated in state space models.

11.2. State space representation in SsfPack*

As discussed earlier in Chapter 9, linear state space models can be represented in the following general format:

$$y_t = Z_t a_t + \varepsilon_t, \qquad\qquad \varepsilon_t \sim \text{NID}(0, H_t) \qquad (11.1)$$

$$a_{t+1} = T_t a_t + R_t \eta_t \qquad\qquad \eta_t \sim \text{NID}(0, Q_t) \qquad (11.2)$$

for $t = 1, \ldots, n$. In SsfPack the matrix representation of state space models is even more compact:

$$\begin{pmatrix} a_{t+1} \\ y_t \end{pmatrix} = \Phi_t a_t + u_t, \qquad u_t \sim \text{NID}(0, \Omega_t) \qquad (11.3)$$

for $t = 1, \ldots, n$, where

$$\Phi_t = \begin{pmatrix} T_t \\ Z_t \end{pmatrix}, \qquad u_t = \begin{pmatrix} \eta_t \\ \varepsilon_t \end{pmatrix} \qquad \text{and} \qquad \Omega_t = \begin{bmatrix} R_t Q_t R_t' & 0 \\ 0 & H_t \end{bmatrix}.$$

The system matrix Φ_t is of order $(m+p) \times m$ and Ω_t is of order $(m+p) \times (m+p)$. The sum of unobserved components (i.e. the prediction of y_t in classical regression terminology) is defined by the $p \times 1$ vector

$$\theta_t = Z_t \alpha_t, \tag{11.4}$$

and is referred to as the *signal*.

The state space formulation is not complete without defining the initial state vector α_1. Generally we assume that

$$\alpha_1 \sim NID(a_1, P_1),$$

where the $m \times 1$ vector a_1 and $m \times m$ matrix P_1 are fixed. In many cases the initial conditions are implied by the model. For example, the unconditional properties of the AR(1) model where $y_t = \alpha_t$ and $\alpha_{t+1} = \phi \alpha_t + \eta_t$ imposes $a_1 = 0$ and $P_1 = \sigma_\eta^2/(1 - \phi^2)$. In cases that the state vector contains regression coefficients or non-stationary processes, the initial state cannot be properly defined and we let $P_1 \rightarrow \infty$ or attach very large values to P_1. In SsfPack, the initial conditions can be defined explicitly by the system matrix Σ that is defined as

$$\Sigma = \begin{pmatrix} P_1 \\ a_1' \end{pmatrix}.$$

The user is free to design the SsfPack state space matrices Φ_t, Ω_t and Σ as long as they are consistent with each other and as long as the implied model is properly specified. For this matter, some basic checks concerning dimensions are carried out by SsfPack but the actual design of the system matrices is the sole responsibility of the user.

The construction of the system matrices for even some basic time series models can be intricate. Therefore, SsfPack offers some basic functions that create the appropriate system matrices for a range of time series models including the standard regression model, the ARIMA model and the structural time series model. For example, the SsfPack routine GetSsfStsm() provides the relevant system matrices for any univariate structural time series model:

```
GetSsfStsm(mStsm, &mPhi, &mOmega, &mSigma);
```

The routine requires one input matrix containing the model information in the following form

$$
\texttt{mStsm} = <\;
\begin{array}{llll}
\texttt{CMP\_LEVEL,} & \sigma_\xi, & 0, & 0; \\
\texttt{CMP\_SLOPE,} & \sigma_\zeta, & 0, & 0; \\
\texttt{CMP\_SEAS\_DUMMY,} & \sigma_\omega, & s, & 0; \\
\texttt{CMP\_IRREG,} & \sigma_\varepsilon, & 0, & 0 >;
\end{array}
$$

The rows in the input matrix may have a different sequential order. However, the resulting state vector is always organised in the sequence level, slope, seasonal and irregular. The first column of matrix mStsm uses predefined constants, and the remaining columns contain real values. The second column is for the standard deviation of the disturbance that drives a particular component. The s in the third column of the CMP_SEAS_DUMMY row is the periodicity of the (dummy) seasonal. The final zero column is an auxiliary column that is used for other possible components in the model. The function GetSsfStsm() returns three system matrices mPhi, mOmega, and mSigma. For example, in the case of a local linear trend model, we have

$$
\texttt{mStsm} = <\;
\begin{array}{llll}
\texttt{CMP\_LEVEL,} & \sigma_\xi, & 0, & 0; \\
\texttt{CMP\_SLOPE,} & \sigma_\zeta, & 0, & 0; \\
\texttt{CMP\_IRREG,} & \sigma_\varepsilon, & 0, & 0 >;
\end{array}
$$

with the returned matrices mPhi, mOmega, and mSigma given by

$$
\Phi_t = \begin{pmatrix} T_t \\ Z_t \end{pmatrix} = \begin{bmatrix} 1 & 1 \\ 0 & 1 \\ 1 & 0 \end{bmatrix}, \quad
\Omega_t = \begin{bmatrix} Q_t & 0 \\ 0 & H_t \end{bmatrix} = \begin{bmatrix} \sigma_\xi^2 & 0 & 0 \\ 0 & \sigma_\zeta^2 & 0 \\ 0 & 0 & \sigma_\varepsilon^2 \end{bmatrix}, \quad
\Sigma = \begin{bmatrix} -1 & 0 \\ 0 & -1 \\ 0 & 0 \end{bmatrix},
$$

respectively, also compare with (11.3). It is implied that the state vector is given by $\alpha_t = (\mu_t, \nu_t)'$. Matrix mSigma determines whether the initialisations of the level and the slope at $t = 1$ are diffuse or not (a minus one indicating that they are diffuse, which is the default).

The following Ox code illustrates how to set up system matrices for the local linear trend model.

```
#include <oxstd.h>
#include <packages/ssfpack/ssfpack.h>

main()
{
    // declare variables
    decl mStsm, mPhi, mOmega, mSigma;
    // set up state space definition matrix local linear trend model
```

```
mStsm = <   CMP_LEVEL, 0.5, 0, 0;
            CMP_SLOPE, 0.3, 0, 0;
            CMP_IRREG, 0.4, 0, 0>;

    // set up system matrices local linear trend model
    GetSsfStsm(mStsm, &mPhi, &mOmega, &mSigma);

    // print state space definition matrix and system matrices
    print("mStsm", mStsm, "mPhi", mPhi, "mOmega", mOmega, "mSigma", mSigma);
}
```

The output of this introductory Ox program is given below.

```
mStsm
        0.00000     0.50000     0.00000     0.00000
        1.0000      0.30000     0.00000     0.00000
        16.000      0.40000     0.00000     0.00000
mPhi
        1.0000      1.0000
        0.00000     1.0000
        1.0000      0.00000
mOmega
        0.25000     0.00000     0.00000
        0.00000     0.090000    0.00000
        0.00000     0.00000     0.16000
mSigma
       -1.0000      0.00000
        0.00000    -1.0000
        0.00000     0.00000
```

Note that the entries on the diagonal of mOmega are equal to the squared entries in the second column of mStsm, as they should be.

In the documentation of SsfPack more illustrations are given of how some standard time series models can be represented in state space using functions such as GetSsfArma() and GetSsfReg(), see Koopman et al. (1999, Section 2). In the next section we show how regression and intervention effects can be incorporated in the model.

11.3. Incorporating regression and intervention effects*

Structural time series models and ARMA models can be represented by time-invariant state space models. However, regression models lead to time-varying models since the explanatory variable x_t is placed in the Z_t matrix of (11.1) while the regression coefficient is part of the state vector (see also Section 8.1). The multiple regression model (5.1) of Chapter 5, with $\mu_t = 0$, is given by

$$y_t = \sum_{j=1}^{k} \beta_j x_{jt} + \varepsilon_t,$$

for $t = 1, \ldots, n$. In state space form, we have the state vector $a_t = (\beta_1, \ldots, \beta_k)'$

$$Z_t = (x_{1t}, \ldots, x_{kt}), \quad T_t = R_t = I, \quad Q_t = 0,$$

where I is the $k \times k$ identity matrix. The system matrix Z_t is therefore time-varying. The three basic SsfPack matrices are not time-varying; they represent fixed values. The SsfPack routines can be informed about the time-variation of mPhi and mOmega via what are called the index matrices mJPhi and mJOmega which have the same dimensions as mPhi and mOmega, respectively. All elements of the index matrices are set equal to -1 as a default. When a particular element of an index matrix is equal to a non-negative integer $(0, 1, 2, \ldots)$, the corresponding element of the system matrix is regarded as time-varying. The time-varying values are placed in a data matrix with n columns. The non-negative value of a particular element in one of the two index matrices indicates the row of the data matrix that contains the time-varying values of the corresponding element of the corresponding system matrix. Since the system matrices need to be known for every t, the data matrix must be a full and known matrix. When a particular system matrix is time-invariant, the corresponding index matrix does not need to be created and can be taken as an empty matrix. In the Ox system, an empty matrix is indicated by <>.

This administration for time-varying system matrices is quite flexible. As long as a data matrix is available that contains the time-varying values of the system matrices, the SsfPack functions can exploit these using the index matrices mJPhi and mJOmega. In practice, this facility will be used most frequently for regression and intervention effects. In case of the standard regression model, the data matrix

$$X = \begin{bmatrix} x_{11} & \cdots & x_{1n} \\ & \vdots & \\ x_{k1} & \cdots & x_{kn} \end{bmatrix}$$

needs to be created and in Ox may be labelled as mX. Some of the explanatory variables may be designed as a particular intervention effect that usually consists of 0 and 1 values. The SsfPack system then further needs the index matrix mJPhi. The function GetSsfReg() creates the three system matrices and the index matrix mJPhi for a given data matrix X, that is

```
GetSsfReg(mX, &mPhi, &mOmega, &mSigma, &mJPhi);
```

To add explanatory and intervention variables in the local linear trend model, the SsfPack function AddSsfReg() can be used. This is illustrated in the following Ox program. It considers the model

$$y_t = \mu_t + \beta x_t + \lambda w_t + \varepsilon_t,$$

where μ_t is modelled as a local linear trend, the explanatory variable x_t is for the log of petrol price and the intervention variable w_t is for the introduction of the seat belt law (as discussed in the illustrations in Chapters 5–7). The program creates a state space model for the state vector $a_t = (\beta, \lambda, \mu_t, \nu_t)'$.

```
#include <oxstd.h>
#include <packages/ssfpack/ssfpack.h>

main()
{
    decl mX, mStsm, mPhi, mOmega, mSigma, mJPhi = <>;

    // set up data matrix with explanatory and intervention variables
    mX = loadmat("logpetrol.dat")' | (constant(0, 1, 169) ~ constant(1, 1, 23));

    // set up state space definition matrix local linear trend model
    mStsm = <   CMP_LEVEL, 0.5, 0, 0;
                CMP_SLOPE, 0.3, 0, 0;
                CMP_IRREG, 0.4, 0, 0>;

    // set up system matrices local linear trend model
    GetSsfStsm(mStsm, &mPhi, &mOmega, &mSigma);
    // add explanatory and intervention variables to system matrices
    AddSsfReg(mX, &mPhi, &mOmega, &mSigma, &mJPhi);

    // print state space definition matrix and system matrices
    print("mStsm", mStsm, "mPhi", mPhi, "mOmega", mOmega);
    print("mSigma", mSigma, "mJPhi", mJPhi);
}
```

The output is:

```
mStsm
        0.00000        0.50000        0.00000        0.00000
        1.0000         0.30000        0.00000        0.00000
        16.000         0.40000        0.00000        0.00000
mPhi
        1.0000         0.00000        0.00000        0.00000
        0.00000        1.0000         0.00000        0.00000
        0.00000        0.00000        1.0000         1.0000
        0.00000        0.00000        0.00000        1.0000
        0.00000        0.00000        1.0000         0.00000
mOmega
        0.00000        0.00000        0.00000        0.00000        0.00000
        0.00000        0.00000        0.00000        0.00000        0.00000
        0.00000        0.00000        0.25000        0.00000        0.00000
        0.00000        0.00000        0.00000        0.090000       0.00000
        0.00000        0.00000        0.00000        0.00000        0.16000
```

```
mSigma
        -1.0000      0.00000      0.00000      0.00000
        0.00000     -1.0000       0.00000      0.00000
        0.00000      0.00000     -1.0000       0.00000
        0.00000      0.00000      0.00000     -1.0000
        0.00000      0.00000      0.00000      0.00000
mJPhi
        -1.0000     -1.0000      -1.0000      -1.0000
        -1.0000     -1.0000      -1.0000      -1.0000
        -1.0000     -1.0000      -1.0000      -1.0000
        -1.0000     -1.0000      -1.0000      -1.0000
        0.00000      1.0000      -1.0000      -1.0000
```

11.4. Estimation of a model in SsfPack*

In the previous section it was shown how the SsfPack system can be
informed about the model that is used for analysis and forecasting.
However, a model can be subject to unknown parameters. For the local
linear trend model, for example, the variances of the level, slope, and
observation disturbances are unknown. They can be randomly chosen
but such values may be of no relevance to the time series that is analysed.
We therefore need to estimate the unknown parameters for a given time
series. In most earlier chapters of this book, the unknown variances and
other parameters are estimated by maximum likelihood. These estimated
values are presented and used in the model for further analysis. In this section we show how such unknown parameters are estimated by maximum
likelihood in practice using the Ox and SsfPack systems.

The likelihood function is the joint density of a set of stochastic variables that are assumed generated by a particular model. When the stochastic variables are observed and available to the researcher, these variables
are treated as realisations and referred to as observations. Furthermore,
the observations are taken as fixed such that the likelihood function
only varies when the parameters change for a given model. In our situation, where the observations consist of a univariate or multivariate time
series, the model can be represented in state space and the parameters
are unknown and need to be estimated. When we have p time series
consisting of n observations each, and when the time series are collected
in a data vector y of order $np \times 1$ and the distributional assumptions are
based on normal density, we have

$$y \sim N(\mu, V),$$

with mean vector μ of order $np \times 1$ and variance matrix V of order $np \times np$.
In a time series context, the observations are subject to serial correlation
such that the variance matrix is a full matrix (whose inverse has a very

special band structure). In this case the log-likelihood function of the $np \times 1$ data vector y is given by

$$\log p(y) = -\frac{np}{2} \log(2\pi) - \frac{1}{2} \log |V| - \frac{1}{2}(y - \mu)'V^{-1}(y - \mu),$$

for a given y and a vector of unknown parameters ψ. The mean vector μ and variance matrix V depend on the parameter vector ψ. When np is large, the dimension of V becomes large and the computations for $\log p(y)$ become cumbersome since $|V|$ (the determinant of matrix V) and its inverse V^{-1} need to be calculated. Given that the model can be represented as a state space model, matrix V has the just mentioned special band structure. This structure of matrix V allows the Kalman filter of Section 8.4 to be used for the computation of $|V|$ and $x'V^{-1}x$ with $x = y - \mu$. More specifically, the log-likelihood function is given by

$$\log L (y|\psi) = -\frac{np}{2} \log (2\pi) - \frac{1}{2} \sum_{t=1}^{n} (\log |F_t| + v_t'F_t^{-1}v_t), \qquad (11.5)$$

where v_t is the one-step ahead prediction error and F_t is its variance for $t = 1, \ldots, n$ (see also Section 8.4).

For a given value of $\psi = \psi^*$, the Kalman filter is used to compute the log-likelihood value $\log L(y|\psi)$. For different values of ψ, the likelihood value is different and we aim to find the value of ψ that produces the maximum likelihood value. This value of ψ is referred to as the maximum likelihood value and is given by

$$\widehat{\psi} = \arg \max_\psi \log L(y|\psi).$$

Numerical optimisation methods exist that maximise $\log L(y|\psi)$ with respect to ψ in a computationally efficient way. In the `Ox` system, the Broyden–Fletcher–Goldfarb–Shannon (BFGS) algorithm is available to maximise the log-likelihood value (11.5). This method of estimation is based on a numerical optimisation method that uses the gradient of the likelihood function with respect to ψ. The gradient is then evaluated at some location for $\psi = \psi^*$ and it provides information about the direction in the search for the optimum of the log-likelihood function. The gradient or *score vector* is defined by

$$\partial_1(\psi) = \frac{\partial \log L(y|\psi)}{\partial \psi}. \qquad (11.6)$$

The score vector can be evaluated numerically (see Section 11.4.2). In Sections 11.4.2 and 11.4.3 an analytical method for the computation of the score vector is also discussed. Further, the EM algorithm is introduced in Section 11.4.4 as an alternative for the BFGS algorithm for estimating parameters in state space models.

11.4.1. *Likelihood evaluation using* SsfLikEx

The SsfPack function SsfLikEx() is provided for the computation of the log-likelihood for given values of the state space matrices:

```
SsfLikEx(&dLogLik, &dVar, mYt, mPhi, mOmega, mSigma);
```

This function returns a 1 to indicate that it is successful, and 0 otherwise. The input arguments are the $p \times n$ data matrix mYt, and the state space model consisting of matrices mPhi, mOmega, and mSigma. The function returns variables that are prefixed by &. These are the variables &dLogLik and &dVar as given by

$$\text{dLogLik} = \log L\,(y|\psi) = -\frac{np}{2} \log\,(2\,\pi) - \frac{1}{2} \sum_{t=1}^{n} \left(\log|F_t| + v_t' F_t^{-1} v_t\right),$$

and

$$\text{dVar} = \frac{1}{np - d} \sum_{t=1}^{n} v_t' F_t^{-1} v_t, \tag{11.7}$$

where n is the number of time points (as before), p is the number of dependent variables in y_t (also as before), and d is the number of diffuse initial elements of the state.

The following Ox code illustrates how to evaluate the value of log-likelihood function (11.5) for given state and observation disturbance variances Ω_t using the SsfPack routine SsfLikEx().

```
#include <oxstd.h>
#include <packages/ssfpack/ssfpack.h>

main()
{
    decl mStsm, mPhi, mOmega, mSigma, mYt, dLogLik, dVar;

    // load Norwegian fatalities, transpose and log()
    mYt = log(loadmat("norway.dat")');

    // set up state space definition matrix local linear trend model
    mStsm = <    CMP_LEVEL, 0.5, 0, 0;
                 CMP_SLOPE, 0.3, 0, 0;
                 CMP_IRREG, 0.4, 0, 0>;

    // set up system matrices local linear trend model
    GetSsfStsm(mStsm, &mPhi, &mOmega, &mSigma);
```

144

```
      // print state space definition matrix and system matrices
      print("mStsm", mStsm, "mPhi", mPhi, "mOmega", mOmega, "mSigma", mSigma);

      //evaluate log-likelihood
      SsfLikEx(&dLogLik, &dVar, mYt, mPhi, mOmega, mSigma);
      print("\ndLogLik = ", dLogLik);
      print("\ndVar    = ", dVar);
}
```

The `main()` function starts off by loading the Norwegian fatalities series in
`mYt`, transposing the column vector into a row vector, and then taking the
logarithm:

```
mYt = log(loadmat("norway.dat")');
```

The ASCII file `norway.dat` has the following format (compare with Appendix B):

```
34 1 // yearly traffic casualties in Norway (1970-2003, 34 observations)
560
533
490
:
312
280
```

Then the state space definition matrix is defined as the local linear trend
model and stored in `mStsm`. Next, the `SsfPack` routine `GetSsfStsm()` is called
to set up system matrices `mPhi`, `mOmega`, and `mSigma`, as before. Then the
`SsfPack` routine `SsfLikEx()` is called to evaluate loglikelihood function
(11.5) (and store the result in `dLogLik`), and to compute scale factor (11.7)
(and store the result in `dVar`). The output of this `Ox` program is as follows.

```
mStsm
        0.00000       0.50000       0.00000       0.00000
        1.0000        0.30000       0.00000       0.00000
        16.000        0.40000       0.00000       0.00000
mPhi
        1.0000        1.0000
        0.00000       1.0000
        1.0000        0.00000
mOmega
        0.25000       0.00000       0.00000
        0.00000       0.090000      0.00000
        0.00000       0.00000       0.16000
mSigma
        -1.0000       0.00000
        0.00000       -1.0000
        0.00000       0.00000

dLogLik = -27.876
dVar    = 0.0152944
```

Thus, for the log of Norwegian traffic casualties (where $p = 1$ since there
is only one dependent variable in this case), and given the present values

145

of the level, slope and observation disturbance variances (which are 0.25, 0.09 and 0.16, respectively), we obtain as output

$$\text{dLogLik} = \log L\,(y|\psi) = -\frac{n}{2}\log\,(2\,\pi) - \frac{1}{2}\sum_{t=3}^{n}\left(\log|F_t| + v_t'F_t^{-1}v_t\right) = -27.876,$$

and

$$\text{dVar} = \frac{1}{n-2}\sum_{t=3}^{n}v_t'F_t^{-1}v_t = 0.0152944.$$

Note that the initial state vector contains two diffuse elements in the local linear trend model and therefore prediction errors are only properly defined from $t = 3$ and onwards.

11.4.2. The score vector

The ith element of the score vector $\partial_1(\psi)$ in (11.6) can be approximated numerically by

$$\partial_1(\psi)_i \approx \frac{\log L\,(y|\psi + \epsilon e_i) - \log L\,(y|\psi - \epsilon e_i)}{2\epsilon}, \qquad \epsilon > 0,$$

where e_i is the ith column of the identity matrix and for some suitably small chosen ϵ. The score vector can also be evaluated analytically. In the case that all parameters in ψ are associated with variances of the state space model, the score vector can be expressed by

$$\begin{aligned}
\partial_1(\psi) = -\frac{1}{2}\frac{\partial}{\partial\psi}\sum_{t=1}^{n}&[\log|H_t| + \log|Q_{t-1}|\\
&+ \text{tr}\left(\left\{\hat{\varepsilon}_t\hat{\varepsilon}_t' + \text{Var}(\varepsilon_t|y)\right\}H_t^{-1}\right)\\
&+ \text{tr}\left(\left\{\hat{\eta}_{t-1}\hat{\eta}_{t-1}' + \text{Var}(\eta_{t-1}|y)\right\}Q_t^{-1}\right)].
\end{aligned} \tag{11.8}$$

Expressions for $\hat{\varepsilon}_t$, $\text{Var}(\varepsilon_t|y)$, $\hat{\eta}_t$ and $\text{Var}(\eta_t|y)$ can be presented in terms of quantities from the Kalman filter and smoothing algorithms, of which more details can be found in Durbin and Koopman (2001, Chapters 4 and 7).

To provide more practical details, the univariate local linear trend model of Chapter 3 is considered. For this model, the vector ψ in (11.8) is taken as

$$\psi = \begin{pmatrix}\psi_1\\\psi_2\\\psi_3\end{pmatrix} = \begin{pmatrix}\frac{1}{2}\log\sigma_\xi^2\\\frac{1}{2}\log\sigma_\zeta^2\\\frac{1}{2}\log\sigma_\varepsilon^2\end{pmatrix} = \begin{pmatrix}\log\sigma_\xi\\\log\sigma_\zeta\\\log\sigma_\varepsilon\end{pmatrix}, \tag{11.9}$$

by noting that $\log a^u = u \log a$. The reason for this reparametrisation is that the BFGS optimisation algorithm yields unconstrained parameter estimates. The reparametrisation ensures non-negative variances that can be recovered by

$$
\begin{pmatrix} \sigma_\xi^2 \\ \sigma_\zeta^2 \\ \sigma_\varepsilon^2 \end{pmatrix} = \exp(2\,\psi).
\tag{11.10}
$$

For this particular choice of ψ, the score vector is given by

$$
\frac{\partial \log L(y|\psi)}{\partial \psi} = -\frac{1}{2} \frac{\partial}{\partial \psi} [n \log \sigma_\varepsilon^2 + (n-1) \log \sigma_\xi^2 + (n-1) \log \sigma_\zeta^2
$$
$$
+ \frac{1}{\sigma_\varepsilon^2} c + \mathrm{tr}\left[B \begin{bmatrix} \frac{1}{\sigma_\xi^2} & 0 \\ 0 & \frac{1}{\sigma_\zeta^2} \end{bmatrix} \right]],
\tag{11.11}
$$

where

$$
c = \sum_{t=1}^{n} \{ \hat{\varepsilon}_t^2 + \mathrm{Var}(\varepsilon_t|y) \}, \qquad \text{(a scalar)},
$$
$$
B = \sum_{t=1}^{n} \{ \hat{\eta}_{t-1} \hat{\eta}_{t-1}' + \mathrm{Var}(\eta_{t-1}|y) \}, \quad \text{(a } 2 \times 2 \text{ matrix)}.
\tag{11.12}
$$

It follows that (11.11) can be simplified into

$$
\partial_1(\psi) = \frac{\partial \log L(y|\psi)}{\partial \psi} = \begin{pmatrix} \dfrac{b_{11}}{\exp(2\psi_1)} - (n-1) \\ \dfrac{b_{22}}{\exp(2\psi_2)} - (n-1) \\ \dfrac{c}{\exp(2\psi_3)} - n \end{pmatrix},
\tag{11.13}
$$

where the scalar b_{ij} is the (i, j) element of B.

The ith element of the score vector (11.13) can also be written as

$$
\partial_1(\psi)_i = \frac{\partial \log L(y|\psi)}{\partial \psi_i} = \frac{1}{2} \mathrm{tr}\left(M \frac{\partial \Omega}{\partial \psi_i} \right),
\tag{11.14}
$$

where

$$
\Omega = \begin{bmatrix} \sigma_\xi^2 & 0 & 0 \\ 0 & \sigma_\zeta^2 & 0 \\ 0 & 0 & \sigma_\varepsilon^2 \end{bmatrix},
$$

and with the diagonal elements of M equal to

$$\begin{pmatrix} \frac{1}{\sigma_\xi^2}\left[\frac{b_{11}}{\sigma_\xi^2}-(n-1)\right] \\ \frac{1}{\sigma_\zeta^2}\left[\frac{b_{22}}{\sigma_\zeta^2}-(n-1)\right] \\ \frac{1}{\sigma_\varepsilon^2}\left[\frac{c}{\sigma_\varepsilon^2}-n\right] \end{pmatrix} = \begin{pmatrix} \frac{1}{\exp(2\psi_1)}\left[\frac{b_{11}}{\exp(2\psi_1)}-(n-1)\right] \\ \frac{1}{\exp(2\psi_2)}\left[\frac{b_{22}}{\exp(2\psi_2)}-(n-1)\right] \\ \frac{1}{\exp(2\psi_3)}\left[\frac{c}{\exp(2\psi_3)}-n\right] \end{pmatrix}. \qquad (11.15)$$

To show that the result in (11.14) is valid, we consider the first element of ψ, that is $\psi_1 = \frac{1}{2}\log\sigma_\xi^2$ and observe that

$$\frac{\partial\sigma_\xi^2}{\partial\psi_1} = 2\sigma_\xi^2 \qquad (11.16)$$

since

$$\frac{\partial\sigma_\xi^2}{\partial\psi_1} = \frac{\partial\exp(2\psi_1)}{\partial\psi_1} = \frac{\partial\exp(u)}{\partial u}\frac{\partial u}{\partial\psi_1} = 2\exp(u) = 2\exp(2\psi_1) = 2\sigma_\xi^2,$$

where $u = 2\psi_1$. Also, it is noticed that

$$\frac{\partial\Omega_t}{\partial\psi_1} = \begin{bmatrix} 2\sigma_\xi^2 & 0 & 0 \\ 0 & 0 & 0 \\ 0 & 0 & 0 \end{bmatrix} = \begin{bmatrix} 2\exp(2\psi_1) & 0 & 0 \\ 0 & 0 & 0 \\ 0 & 0 & 0 \end{bmatrix}.$$

The first element of (11.14) is then equal to

$$\partial_1(\psi)_1 = \frac{\partial\log L(y|\psi)}{\partial\psi_1} = \frac{1}{2}\mathrm{tr}\left(M\frac{\partial\Omega_t}{\partial\psi_1}\right)$$

$$= \frac{1}{2}\left(\frac{1}{\exp(2\psi_1)}\left[\frac{b_{11}}{\exp(2\psi_1)}-(n-1)\right]\right)(2\exp(2\psi_1))$$

$$= \frac{b_{11}}{\exp(2\psi_1)} - (n-1)$$

and is identical to the first element of the score vector (11.13), as is required. The same arguments apply to the second and third elements of ψ. Similar results apply for other models as well.

The SsfPack function SsfLikScoEx() operates in a similar way as the function that evaluates the likelihood function SsfLikEx() but additionally it also outputs matrix M in (11.14). The function call is

```
SsfLikScoEx(&dLogLik, &dVar, &mSco, mYt, mPhi, mOmega, mSigma);
```

where mSco represents matrix M. The same Ox code as in the previous section can be used to illustrate the SsfLikScoEx() function.

```
#include <oxstd.h>
#include <packages/ssfpack/ssfpack.h>

main()
{
    decl mStsm, mPhi, mOmega, mSigma, mYt, dLogLik, dVar, mSco;

    ...

    //evaluate log-likelihood and matrix M
    SsfLikScoEx(&dLogLik, &dVar, &mSco, mYt, mPhi, mOmega, mSigma);
    print("\ndLogLik = ", dLogLik);
    print("\ndVar    = ", dVar);
    print("\nmSco    = ", mSco);
}
```

The final part of this code produces the output

```
dLogLik = -27.876
dVar    = 0.0152944
mSco    =
      -43.455       21.727       0.00000
       21.727      -75.999       0.00000
       0.00000      0.00000     -86.294
```

11.4.3. *Numerical maximisation of likelihood in* `Ox`

Different methods of numerical optimisation are available in `Ox`. For our purposes, the most effective methods are the ones that use gradient information from the likelihood function for ψ. During the search to the optimum, the gradient or score vector (11.6) is evaluated at some location for $\psi = \psi^*$ to provide information about the direction in the search to the optimum of the log-likelihood function. The score vector can be evaluated numerically or analytically. In practice, it does not make much difference how the score vector is evaluated. However, analytical methods are usually more efficient from a computational perspective.

Given some trial value $\tilde{\psi}$ for ψ, the quasi-Newton step provides a revised value $\tilde{\psi}^+$ and is given by

$$\tilde{\psi}^+ = \tilde{\psi} + sG \left. \partial_1(\psi) \right|_{\psi=\tilde{\psi}}, \tag{11.17}$$

where the score vector contains the individual directions towards the optimum, matrix G modifies these directions and s is a scalar that determines the step size. Matrix G is usually determined by the second order derivative or Hessian matrix

$$\partial_2(\psi) = \frac{\partial^2 \log L(y|\psi)}{\partial \psi \partial \psi'} \tag{11.18}$$

but it can also be based on another appropriately chosen matrix, see Durbin and Koopman (2001, p.143). The `MaxBFGS` function in `Ox` is based

149

on this quasi-Newton algorithm. The score vector and matrix G can be provided explicitly although this is not needed.

In summary, the optimisation algorithm consists of the following basic steps:

1. Initialise parameter vector $\psi = \psi^*$, as in (11.9).

2. Apply the Kalman filter and smoothing algorithms to obtain matrix M and thus the score vector (11.14) for $\psi = \psi^*$.

3. Use (11.17) to obtain new values for ψ given by ψ^+. Replace ψ^* by ψ^+ and go to step 2 until the value of log-likelihood function (11.5) no longer improves.

In Section 11.4.5 Ox code is provided to give an illustrative example of how this method works in practice.

11.4.4. The EM algorithm

The EM algorithm is a maximum likelihood estimation procedure that consists of two steps: the E(xpectation)-step and the M(aximisation)-step. The two steps are repeated many times (EMEMEMEM ...) until parameter estimates have converged. In the context of state space models, the EM algorithm is a recursive method to obtain maximum likelihood estimates for unknown parameters in the system matrices Φ_t and Ω_t of the SsfPack model, see Durbin and Koopman (2001, p. 143) for more background. A simple method for unknown and time-invariant variances in Ω is given below.

For the local linear trend model, the following EM algorithm can be considered for the estimation of ψ which is now defined as

$$\psi = \begin{pmatrix} \psi_1 \\ \psi_2 \\ \psi_3 \end{pmatrix} = \begin{pmatrix} \sigma_\xi^2 \\ \sigma_\zeta^2 \\ \sigma_\varepsilon^2 \end{pmatrix}. \tag{11.19}$$

1. Initialise parameter vector $\psi = \psi^*$ in (11.19).

2. E-step: Apply the Kalman filter and smoothing algorithms for $\psi = \psi^*$ to obtain matrix M and thus scalar c and matrix B as defined in (11.12).

3. M-step: Solve $\partial_1(\psi) = 0$ with $\partial_1(\psi)$ given by (11.13) with c and B obtained from the previous E-step. For the local linear trend model,

we have

$$\psi_1^+ = \frac{b_{11}}{n-1}, \qquad \psi_2^+ = \frac{b_{22}}{n-1},$$

and

$$\psi_3^+ = \frac{c}{n}.$$

4. Replace ψ^* by ψ^+ and go to step 2 until the value of log-likelihood function (11.5) no longer improves.

The advantages of the EM algorithm are that it guarantees non-negativity of the estimated hyperparameters, and that it satisfies monotone convergence. However, convergence can be extremely slow, especially when there are many parameters to be estimated. Although the BFGS algorithm does not necessarily satisfy monotone convergence, it is usually much faster than the EM algorithm. A mixture of the two methods, where first the EM algorithm is used and next the BFGS algorithm is considered, often leads to an effective estimation method.

11.4.5. *Some illustrations in* Ox

To illustrate the estimation methods we return to Section 2.3 where the parameters of the local level model are estimated for the Norwegian fatalities data. The log-likelihood function is evaluated by the SsfPack function SsfLikEx() and the log-likelihood function is numerically maximised using the Ox routine MaxBFGS(). An example of Ox code for this approach to maximum likelihood estimation is given by

```
...
static decl s_mY, s_cT;                // data (1 x n) and n
static decl s_mStsm, s_vVarCmp;        // matrices for state space model

SetStsmModel(const vP)
{
    s_mStsm = < CMP_LEVEL, 0.5, 0, 0;
                CMP_IRREG,   1, 0, 0>;
    decl vr = exp(2.0 * vP);
    s_vVarCmp =          vr[0] | vr[1];
}
LogLikStsm(const vY, const pdLik, const pdVar)
{
    decl mphi, momega, msigma, ret_val;
    GetSsfStsm(s_mStsm, &mphi, &momega, &msigma);
    momega = diag(s_vVarCmp);          // create Omega from s_vVarCmp
    return = SsfLikEx(pdLik, pdVar, vY, mphi, momega, msigma);
}
LogLikScoStsm(const vY, const pdLik, const pvSco)
{
```

151

```
      decl mphi, momega, msigma, msco, ret_val, dvar, vs;
      GetSsfStsm(s_mStsm, &mphi, &momega, &msigma);
      momega = diag(s_vVarCmp);
      ret_val = SsfLikScoEx(pdLik, &dvar, &msco, vY, mphi, momega, msigma);
      vs = (diagonal(msco)' .* s_vVarCmp);
      pvSco[0][0:1] = vs[0:1] / s_cT;
      pdLik[0] /= s_cT;
      return ret_val;
}
Likelihood(const vP, const pdLik, const pvSco, const pmHes)
{
      decl ret_val, dvar;
      SetStsmModel(vP);
      return pvSco ?
          LogLikScoStsm(s_mY, pdLik, pvSco) : LogLikStsm(s_mY, pdLik, &dvar);
}
InitialPar()
{
      decl dlik, dvar, vp = log(<0.5; 1>);
      SetStsmModel(vp);
      LogLikStsm(s_mY, &dlik, &dvar);
      return vp + 0.5 * log(dvar);
}
MaxLik()
{
      decl vp, dlik, ir;

      vp = InitialPar();
      MaxControl(10, 1, 1);
      ir = MaxBFGS(Likelihood, &vp, &dlik, 0, FALSE);
          ...

}
```

This code is a standard setup for the estimation of variances in state space models. Here the analytical score function is evaluated. The Ox function `Likelihood()` always returns the likelihood value at `vP`, where `vP` is the parameter vector defined as ψ in the previous sections. When an address is given for variable `pvSco`, it also computes the analytical score function. The Ox function `MaxLik()` produces the output that is discussed in Section 2.3. The line

```
      vs = (diagonal(msco)' .* s_vVarCmp);
```

in the Ox function `LogLikScoStsm()` represents the computations

$$\partial(\psi)_1 = \frac{1}{2}\text{tr}\left(M\frac{\partial\Omega_t}{\partial\psi_1}\right), \qquad \partial(\psi)_2 = \frac{1}{2}\text{tr}\left(M\frac{\partial\Omega_t}{\partial\psi_2}\right),$$

where $\psi_1 = \frac{1}{2}\log\sigma_\xi^2$ and $\psi_2 = \frac{1}{2}\log\sigma_\varepsilon^2$, see Section 11.4.2. Note that the program variable `msco` represents the matrix M.

The EM algorithm for estimating the two variances σ_ξ^2 and σ_ε^2 of the local level model can also be implemented in a straightforward way in Ox. An example of an Ox implementation of the EM algorithm is

```
EM()
{
      decl vp, dLikold, dLik, dVar, iter, maxiter = 100;
      decl mphi, momega, msigma, msco, vs;
```

```
s_mStsm = < CMP_LEVEL, 0.5, 0, 0;
            CMP_IRREG,   1, 0, 0>;
GetSsfStsm(s_mStsm, &mphi, &momega, &msigma);
s_vPar = diagonal(momega)';
SsfLikScoEx(&dLikold, &dVar, &msco, s_mY, mphi, momega, msigma);   // E-step
s_vPar *= dVar; // initial parameter values

for(iter=0; iter <= maxiter; ++iter)
{
        vs = (diagonal(msco)' .* s_vPar); // score
        s_vPar = ((s_vPar .* vs) ./ (s_cT-1 | s_cT)) + s_vPar;         // M-step
        momega = diag(s_vPar); // new variance matrix

        SsfLikScoEx(&dLik, &dVar, &msco, s_mY, mphi, momega, msigma); // E-step
        dLik /= s_cT;
        if(fabs((dLik - dLikold)/dLikold) < 10^(-12))
        {
            print("\nConvergence in iteration ", iter);
            print("\nloglikelihood = ", dLik);
            print("\nparameter vector = ", s_vPar);
            return TRUE;
            break;
        }
        dLikold = dLik;
}
return FALSE;
}
```

Since

$$
\texttt{s\_vPar} = \begin{pmatrix} \sigma_\xi^2 \\ \sigma_\varepsilon^2 \end{pmatrix}
$$

and

$$
\texttt{diagonal(msco)} = \begin{pmatrix} \frac{1}{\sigma_\xi^2}\left[\frac{b_{11}}{\sigma_\xi^2} - (n-1)\right] \\ \frac{1}{\sigma_\varepsilon^2}\left[\frac{c}{\sigma_\varepsilon^2} - n\right] \end{pmatrix},
$$

the lines

```
vs = (diagonal(msco)' .* s_vPar); // score
s_vPar = ((s_vPar .* vs) ./ (s_cT-1 | s_cT)) + s_vPar;         // M-step
```

first result in

$$
\texttt{vs} = \begin{pmatrix} \frac{1}{\sigma_\xi^2}\left[\frac{b_{11}}{\sigma_\xi^2} - (n-1)\right] \\ \frac{1}{\sigma_\varepsilon^2}\left[\frac{c}{\sigma_\varepsilon^2} - n\right] \end{pmatrix} \times \begin{pmatrix} \sigma_\xi^2 \\ \sigma_\varepsilon^2 \end{pmatrix} = \begin{pmatrix} \frac{b_{11}}{\sigma_\xi^2} - (n-1) \\ \frac{c}{\sigma_\varepsilon^2} - n \end{pmatrix},
$$

153

and then in

$$
\texttt{s\_vPar} = \left[\begin{pmatrix} \sigma_\xi^2 \\ \sigma_\varepsilon^2 \end{pmatrix} \times \begin{pmatrix} \frac{b_{11}}{\sigma_\xi^2} - (n-1) \\ \frac{c}{\sigma_\varepsilon^2} - n \end{pmatrix} \times \begin{pmatrix} \frac{1}{n-1} \\ \frac{1}{n} \end{pmatrix} \right] + \begin{pmatrix} \sigma_\xi^2 \\ \sigma_\varepsilon^2 \end{pmatrix} = \begin{pmatrix} \frac{b_{11}}{n-1} \\ \frac{c}{n} \end{pmatrix},
$$

as mentioned in step 3 of the EM algorithm in Section 11.4.4.

When applied to the Norwegian fatalities data discussed in Section 2.3, the output is given by

```
Convergence in iteration 72
loglikelihood = 0.846862
parameter vector = 0.0047030
                   0.0032682
```

The parameter estimates are very close to the ones obtained in Section 2.3 where the BFGS algorithm with analytical evaluation of the score vector is used for the maximisation of the likelihood.

11.5. Prediction, filtering, and smoothing*

Once the unknown parameters are estimated, it can be of interest to investigate the implied components such as trend, seasonal and irregular. In $\texttt{SsfPack}$ some functions are provided for the prediction, filtering and smoothing of the state vector, see Section 8.4. The most useful function for this purpose is $\texttt{SsfMomentEstEx()}$ that outputs the estimates of the state vector and their variances:

$$
\widehat{a}_{it} = \mathrm{E}(a_{it}|D), \qquad V_{it} = \mathrm{Var}(a_{it}|D),
$$

where a_{it} is the ith element of the state vector a_t $(i = 1, \ldots, m)$ and D refers to a data set. For prediction (ST_PRED) we have $D = \{y_1, \ldots, y_{t-1}\}$, for filtering (ST_FIL) we have $D = \{y_1, \ldots, y_t\}$ and for smoothing (ST_SMO) we have $D = \{y_1, \ldots, y_n\}$. The signal of the model is defined by the $p \times 1$ vector $\theta_t = Z_t a_t$ in (11.4). $\texttt{SsfMomentEstEx()}$ also outputs the estimates concerning the signal, that is

$$
\widehat{\theta}_{jt} = Z_{jt}\widehat{a}_t = Z_{jt}\mathrm{E}(a_t|D), \qquad \Theta_{jt} = Z_{jt}\mathrm{Var}(a_t|D)Z_{jt}',
$$

where θ_{jt} is the jth element of the signal θ_t and Z_{jt} is the jth row of the matrix Z_t $(j = 1, \ldots, p)$. The output of the function $\texttt{SsfMomentEstEx()}$ is the matrix

$$
\begin{bmatrix}
\widehat{a}_{11} & \cdots & \widehat{a}_{m1} & \widehat{\theta}_{11} & \cdots & \widehat{\theta}_{p1} & V_{11} & \cdots & V_{m1} & \Theta_{11} & \cdots & \Theta_{p1} \\
& \vdots & & & & & & & & & & \\
\widehat{a}_{1n} & \cdots & \widehat{a}_{mn} & \widehat{\theta}_{1n} & \cdots & \widehat{\theta}_{pn} & V_{1n} & \cdots & V_{mn} & \Theta_{1n} & \cdots & \Theta_{pn}
\end{bmatrix}'
.
$$

The next Ox program is to illustrate the SsfMomentEstEx() function. It is based on the earlier Ox program for the Norwegian casualties discussed in Section 11.4.1 where we add the following lines:

```
#include <oxstd.h>
#include <packages/ssfpack/ssfpack.h>

main()
{
    decl mStsm, mPhi, mOmega, mSigma, mYt, dLogLik, dVar, mSco;

    ...

    // prediction, filtering and smoothing
    decl mPrd, mFil, mSmo;
    SsfMomentEstEx(ST_PRED, &mPrd, mYt, mPhi, mOmega, mSigma);
    SsfMomentEstEx(ST_FIL, &mFil, mYt, mPhi, mOmega, mSigma);
    SsfMomentEstEx(ST_SMO, &mSmo, mYt, mPhi, mOmega, mSigma);
    print("\nPrediction, filtering and smoothing of LEVEL");
    print("\nwith corresponding s.e.'s (last 3 columns)\n");
    print((mPrd[0][] | mFil[0][] | mSmo[0][] | sqrt(mPrd[3][] | mFil[3][]
        | mSmo[3][]))');
    print("\nPrediction, filtering and smoothing of SLOPE");
    print("\nwith corresponding s.e.'s (last 3 columns)\n");
    print((mPrd[1][] | mFil[1][] | mSmo[1][] | sqrt(mPrd[4][] | mFil[4][]
        | mSmo[4][]))');
}
```

The final part of this code produces the output

```
Prediction, filtering and smoothing of LEVEL
with corresponding s.e.'s (last 3 columns)
        0.00000        6.3279        6.3202        0.00000      0.40000      0.36146
        6.3279        6.2785        6.2738        0.64031      0.40000      0.30439
        6.2291        6.1980        6.2243        1.1790       0.37879      0.30308
        6.1302        6.2200        6.2330        0.93753      0.36791      0.30287
          :
        5.7589        5.8185        5.7745        0.84393      0.36146      0.30287
        5.8506        5.6597        5.6835        0.84393      0.36146      0.30308
        5.6166        5.7198        5.7026        0.84393      0.36146      0.30439
        5.7174        5.6499        5.6499        0.84393      0.36146      0.36146

Prediction, filtering and smoothing of SLOPE
with corresponding s.e.'s (last 3 columns)
        0.00000        0.00000       -0.034245       0.00000      0.00000      0.37254
        0.00000       -0.049415      -0.029871       0.30000      0.81240      0.31196
       -0.049415      -0.067773      -0.018449       0.86603      0.56231      0.28773
       -0.067773      -0.026818      -0.016803       0.63733      0.50155      0.27992
          :
        0.0086568      0.032095      -0.026126       0.56461      0.47831      0.28773
        0.032095      -0.043014      -0.020438       0.56461      0.47831      0.31196
       -0.043014      -0.0024259     -0.028962       0.56461      0.47831      0.37254
       -0.0024259     -0.028962      -0.028962       0.56461      0.47831      0.47831
```

The output reveals various features of prediction, filtering and smoothing. The predictive estimates, including their variances, are only valid from $t = 3$ in the case of the local linear trend model. The output for $t = 1$ and $t = 2$ is not relevant for prediction. The filtered estimates are valid from $t = 2$ and the smoothed estimates are valid for all t. The final filtered estimates for $t = n$ are equivalent to the smoothed estimates at $t = n$.

We end this chapter by noting that the Ox and SsfPack code for performing all the analyses discussed in the book – as well as the data files – can be downloaded from http://staff.feweb.vu.nl/Koopman and from http://www.ssfpack.com.

12

Conclusions

In Chapters 2–7 a practical stepwise approach to univariate time series analysis by state space methods was presented. First, those state components were discussed that can be used to obtain an adequate description of the time series at hand: the level, the slope and the seasonal. For the log of the annual number of traffic fatalities in Norway, the local level model provides a good description of the data, while the smooth trend model was found to provide a good description of the same type of data in Finland. In the case of the log of the monthly number of drivers killed or seriously injured in the UK in the period January 1969 to December 1984, the model consisting of a stochastic level and a deterministic seasonal was found to give the best description of this time series. For the quarterly price changes in the UK in the period of 1950–2001 this was a stochastic level and stochastic seasonal model.

Next, it was illustrated how other components can be added to the model in order to obtain explanations for the time series: explanatory and intervention variables. The log of the petrol price and the introduction of the seat belt law in February 1983 in the UK are both significant predictors of the UK development in drivers killed or seriously injured. There is a negative relation between petrol price and number of drivers KSI. More specifically, keeping all other components constant a 1% increase in petrol price results in a 0.28% reduction in the numbers of drivers KSI. This could be explained by the fact that higher petrol prices result in a reduction of the number of vehicles circulating in traffic. The significant value of the regression coefficient for the intervention variable indicates that the introduction of the seat belt law in February 1983 in the UK resulted in a reduction of 21.3% in the number of drivers KSI. The addition of two pulse intervention variables to the UK quarterly price changes series also improved the fit of the model as well as the results of the diagnostic tests on the residuals.

As discussed in the present book, whether a state component should be treated stochastically or deterministically can be determined by evaluating the variance estimate of the disturbance(s) associated with the state component. If the variance of the stochastic component is very small (i.e. almost zero), then the component should be handled deterministically, since this leads to a more parsimonious model. This can be verified by comparing the values of the Akaike information criterion of the two models with stochastic and with deterministic component. The AIC for the model with a deterministic component should be somewhat smaller than the one with a stochastic component. In the present book, this was found to be the case for the seasonal component of the UK drivers KSI series for example.

A useful property of state space methods is that fully deterministic state space models can be treated as classical linear regression models. This makes it particularly easy to evaluate the benefits obtained from analysing time series with stochastic state space models instead of classical regression models. The first important advantage of state space methods over classical regression is that the former methods usually result in a much better fit to the data. At least as important is the fact that state space methods explicitly take the time dependencies between the observations of a time series into account. This leads to residuals that are much closer to independent random values than in classical linear regression. As discussed in the present book, significance tests for the contributions of explanatory and intervention variables to the models are therefore much more reliable in state space methods than in classical regression analysis of time series data.

In Chapter 8, a general notation for univariate state space models was presented, as well as a number of alternative options for handling explanatory and intervention variables. Moreover, the possibility of establishing confidence intervals for each modelled state component was discussed together with the handling of missing data and the estimation of unknown future observations. Chapter 8 further presented diagnostic test statistics for time series residuals (independence, homoscedasticity and normality) and introduced the one-step ahead prediction error and its variance. In Chapter 9 multivariate time series analysis by state space methods was introduced.

In Chapter 10 the popular Box–Jenkins approach to time series analysis was discussed, allowing for an evaluation of the relative merits of

Box–Jenkins and state space methods. This evaluation turned out in favour of time series analysis by state space methods, because the latter methods explicitly model the trend and seasonal in a series (hence the name structural time series models), and easily handle missing data, explanatory variables and multivariate time series while this is more intricate in ARIMA modelling.

Finally, in Chapter 11 it was shown how to perform a time series analysis based on models discussed in Chapters 1–9 in Ox and SsfPack.

With this book, we not only hope to have provided an easier access to the understanding of the exciting new field of state space time series analysis than can be found in the current literature on this subject, but also to have convinced researchers of the substantial advantages of using this approach in comparison with other available techniques for the analysis of time series data.

12.1. Further reading

This book has presented a complete introduction to the basic concepts of state space and unobserved components time series models. We have restricted ourselves to review basic examples of univariate and multivariate linear Gaussian time series models. We have discussed a number of interesting structural time series models with trend and seasonal components. However, it should be emphasized that all linear time series models can be formulated in state space. A classic monograph on unobserved components models (theory and methods) is Harvey (1989). This book shows that the unobserved-component model is not restricted to the basic decomposition of trend plus seasonal plus irregular. Other components such as cycles and ARMA processes can be incorporated in the model as well. In economics, the cycle component may capture the business cycle fluctuations which play an important role in macroeconomic policy decision-making. Furthermore, unobserved components can be considered in more general settings than the univariate model. For example, Harvey (1989) presents multivariate generalisations, nonlinear and non-Gaussian extensions and continuous-time formulations of the structural time series model. The observation equation in the state space model can also be represented as a sum of unobserved components which are modelled as stationary and nonstationary dynamic processes. Such models are sometimes referred to as RegComponent models, see Bell (2004). It is convenient that state space models can include such a wide range of time series models.

Furthermore, the methods associated with state space (Kalman filter, smoothing algorithm) are discussed but the equations and their derivations are not given. Although the details are not given, the reader should have a clear idea of the purpose of the various algorithms related to the Kalman filter. Those who are interested in a more technical exposition of the Kalman filter and associated smoothing algorithms are referred to the textbook of Durbin and Koopman (2001, Part I) but also classic references such as Anderson and Moore (1979), Harvey (1989), and West and Harrison (1997) provide good treatments. Issues such as numerically stable implementations, exact diffuse initialisations of non-stationary processes and efficient treatments of multivariate models are covered in the more recent literature and reviewed in Durbin and Koopman (2001, Part I). From a closer inspection of the algorithms, it will emerge that the methods are quite flexible in their handling of messy features such as missing observations, irregular spacing, treatment of outliers and breaks, special effects; see Harvey et al. (1998) for a detailed discussion of treatments of messy aspects in the analysis of time series.

There are various textbooks that treat linear Gaussian state space models and methods. A few examples are Brockwell and Davis (1987), Hamilton (1994), West and Harrison (1997), and Shumway and Stoffer (2000). This book has given an introduction for which only an introductory course in regression analysis is required. A more complete introduction in the statistical analysis of time series that includes state space and unobserved components is presented in, for example, the books of Harvey (1993) and Brockwell and Davis (2002).

An up-to-date treatment of state space methods is presented by Durbin and Koopman (2001, Part I). The class of linear Gaussian models can be regarded as restrictive when one is dealing with non-standard time series processes for binary, count and categorical data. Furthermore, time series from fields such as engineering, biostatistics and financial markets have features that cannot be treated by linear Gaussian processes. In such situations, observation and state variables require model formulations that incorporate nonlinear and/or non-Gaussian dynamic processes. The range of such models is large and it is a challenging task to develop

160

methods for the time series analysis of nonlinear and non-Gaussian time series models including parameter estimation and signal extraction. This introductory book has shown that such methods are widely available for linear Gaussian time series but more advanced methods are needed for the analysis of more general models. This research area is very active. Some recent textbook references are Akaike and Kitagawa (1999), Doucet et al. (2000), and Durbin and Koopman (2001, Part II).

UK drivers KSI and petrol price

date	drivers KSI	petrol price	date	drivers KSI	petrol price
1969-JAN	1687	0.1030	1972-MAY	1976	0.0887
1969-FEB	1508	0.1024	1972-JUN	1853	0.0882
1969-MAR	1507	0.1021	1972-JUL	1965	0.0889
1969-APR	1385	0.1009	1972-AUG	1689	0.0882
1969-MAY	1632	0.1010	1972-SEP	1778	0.0889
1969-JUN	1511	0.1006	1972-OCT	1976	0.0877
1969-JUL	1559	0.1038	1972-NOV	2397	0.0874
1969-AUG	1630	0.1041	1972-DEC	2654	0.0870
1969-SEP	1579	0.1038	1973-JAN	2097	0.0864
1969-OCT	1653	0.1030	1973-FEB	1963	0.0859
1969-NOV	2152	0.1027	1973-MAR	1677	0.0854
1969-DEC	2148	0.1020	1973-APR	1941	0.0838
1970-JAN	1752	0.1013	1973-MAY	2003	0.0846
1970-FEB	1765	0.1007	1973-JUN	1813	0.0841
1970-MAR	1717	0.1001	1973-JUL	2012	0.0838
1970-APR	1558	0.0986	1973-AUG	1912	0.0835
1970-MAY	1575	0.0983	1973-SEP	2084	0.0828
1970-JUN	1520	0.0981	1973-OCT	2080	0.0812
1970-JUL	1805	0.0973	1973-NOV	2118	0.0829
1970-AUG	1800	0.0974	1973-DEC	2150	0.0942
1970-SEP	1719	0.0974	1974-JAN	1608	0.0924
1970-OCT	2008	0.0964	1974-FEB	1503	0.1082
1970-NOV	2242	0.0957	1974-MAR	1548	0.1072
1970-DEC	2478	0.0951	1974-APR	1382	0.1140
1971-JAN	2030	0.0967	1974-MAY	1731	0.1125
1971-FEB	1655	0.0961	1974-JUN	1798	0.1113
1971-MAR	1693	0.0954	1974-JUL	1779	0.1103
1971-APR	1623	0.0947	1974-AUG	1887	0.1082
1971-MAY	1805	0.0941	1974-SEP	2004	0.1070
1971-JUN	1746	0.0935	1974-OCT	2077	0.1049
1971-JUL	1795	0.0930	1974-NOV	2092	0.1194
1971-AUG	1926	0.0928	1974-DEC	2051	0.1176
1971-SEP	1619	0.0927	1975-JAN	1577	0.1330
1971-OCT	1992	0.0923	1975-FEB	1356	0.1308
1971-NOV	2233	0.0917	1975-MAR	1652	0.1283
1971-DEC	2192	0.0913	1975-APR	1382	0.1235
1972-JAN	2080	0.0907	1975-MAY	1519	0.1186
1972-FEB	1768	0.0903	1975-JUN	1421	0.1163
1972-MAR	1835	0.0900	1975-JUL	1442	0.1152
1972-APR	1569	0.0891	1975-AUG	1543	0.1145

date	drivers KSI	petrol price	date	drivers KSI	petrol price
1975-SEP	1656	0.1135	1980-MAY	1453	0.1106
1975-OCT	1561	0.1119	1980-JUN	1522	0.1119
1975-NOV	1905	0.1106	1980-JUL	1460	0.1097
1975-DEC	2199	0.1153	1980-AUG	1552	0.1082
1976-JAN	1473	0.1138	1980-SEP	1548	0.1063
1976-FEB	1655	0.1123	1980-OCT	1827	0.1042
1976-MAR	1407	0.1118	1980-NOV	1737	0.1019
1976-APR	1395	0.1096	1980-DEC	1941	0.1028
1976-MAY	1530	0.1084	1981-JAN	1474	0.1048
1976-JUN	1309	0.1079	1981-FEB	1458	0.1040
1976-JUL	1526	0.1091	1981-MAR	1542	0.1167
1976-AUG	1327	0.1076	1981-APR	1404	0.1152
1976-SEP	1627	0.1062	1981-MAY	1522	0.1130
1976-OCT	1748	0.1063	1981-JUN	1385	0.1139
1976-NOV	1958	0.1048	1981-JUL	1641	0.1191
1976-DEC	2274	0.1035	1981-AUG	1510	0.1245
1977-JAN	1648	0.1014	1981-SEP	1681	0.1232
1977-FEB	1401	0.1004	1981-OCT	1938	0.1207
1977-MAR	1411	0.0989	1981-NOV	1868	0.1210
1977-APR	1403	0.1025	1981-DEC	1726	0.1170
1977-MAY	1394	0.1030	1982-JAN	1456	0.1128
1977-JUN	1520	0.1022	1982-FEB	1445	0.1081
1977-JUL	1528	0.0998	1982-MAR	1456	0.1088
1977-AUG	1643	0.0926	1982-APR	1365	0.1113
1977-SEP	1515	0.0918	1982-MAY	1487	0.1113
1977-OCT	1685	0.0907	1982-JUN	1558	0.1155
1977-NOV	2000	0.0900	1982-JUL	1488	0.1148
1977-DEC	2215	0.0893	1982-AUG	1684	0.1172
1978-JAN	1956	0.0884	1982-SEP	1594	0.1191
1978-FEB	1462	0.0884	1982-OCT	1850	0.1180
1978-MAR	1563	0.0868	1982-NOV	1998	0.1174
1978-APR	1459	0.0850	1982-DEC	2079	0.1170
1978-MAY	1446	0.0846	1983-JAN	1494	0.1126
1978-JUN	1622	0.0844	1983-FEB	1057	0.1137
1978-JUL	1657	0.0844	1983-MAR	1218	0.1131
1978-AUG	1638	0.0836	1983-APR	1168	0.1185
1978-SEP	1643	0.0834	1983-MAY	1236	0.1180
1978-OCT	1683	0.0827	1983-JUN	1076	0.1177
1978-NOV	2050	0.0852	1983-JUL	1174	0.1201
1978-DEC	2262	0.0848	1983-AUG	1139	0.1194
1979-JAN	1813	0.0845	1983-SEP	1427	0.1189
1979-FEB	1445	0.0854	1983-OCT	1487	0.1185
1979-MAR	1762	0.0876	1983-NOV	1483	0.1180
1979-APR	1461	0.0904	1983-DEC	1513	0.1177
1979-MAY	1556	0.0908	1984-JAN	1357	0.1178
1979-JUN	1431	0.1087	1984-FEB	1165	0.1148
1979-JUL	1427	0.1141	1984-MAR	1282	0.1157
1979-AUG	1554	0.1130	1984-APR	1110	0.1154
1979-SEP	1645	0.1113	1984-MAY	1297	0.1148
1979-OCT	1653	0.1091	1984-JUN	1185	0.1148
1979-NOV	2016	0.1077	1984-JUL	1222	0.1149
1979-DEC	2207	0.1076	1984-AUG	1284	0.1148
1980-JAN	1665	0.1038	1984-SEP	1444	0.1141
1980-FEB	1361	0.1071	1984-OCT	1575	0.1165
1980-MAR	1506	0.1074	1984-NOV	1737	0.1160
1980-APR	1360	0.1117	1984-DEC	1763	0.1161

Road traffic fatalities in Norway and Finland

date	Norway	Finland
1970	560	1055
1971	533	1143
1972	490	1156
1973	511	1086
1974	509	865
1975	539	910
1976	471	804
1977	442	709
1978	434	610
1979	437	650
1980	362	551
1981	338	555
1982	401	569
1983	409	604
1984	407	541
1985	402	541
1986	452	612
1987	398	581
1988	378	653
1989	381	734
1990	332	649
1991	323	632
1992	325	601
1993	281	484
1994	283	480
1995	305	441
1996	255	404
1997	303	438
1998	352	400
1999	304	431
2000	341	396
2001	275	433
2002	312	415
2003	280	379

Source: IRTAD.

APPENDIX C

UK front and rear seat passengers KSI

date	front seat	rear seat	travel kms	date	front seat	rear seat	travel kms
1969-JAN	867	269	9059	1972-MAY	1075	434	13885
1969-FEB	825	265	7685	1972-JUN	1121	486	14088
1969-MAR	806	319	9963	1972-JUL	1190	569	16932
1969-APR	814	407	10955	1972-AUG	1058	523	16164
1969-MAY	991	454	11823	1972-SEP	939	418	14883
1969-JUN	945	427	12391	1972-OCT	1074	452	13532
1969-JUL	1004	522	13460	1972-NOV	1089	462	12220
1969-AUG	1091	536	14055	1972-DEC	1208	497	12025
1969-SEP	958	405	12106	1973-JAN	903	354	11692
1969-OCT	850	437	11372	1973-FEB	916	347	11081
1969-NOV	1109	434	9834	1973-MAR	787	276	13745
1969-DEC	1113	437	9267	1973-APR	1114	472	14382
1970-JAN	925	316	9130	1973-MAY	1014	487	14391
1970-FEB	903	311	8933	1973-JUN	1022	505	15597
1970-MAR	1006	351	11000	1973-JUL	1114	619	16834
1970-APR	892	362	10733	1973-AUG	1132	640	17282
1970-MAY	990	486	12912	1973-SEP	1111	559	15779
1970-JUN	866	429	12926	1973-OCT	1008	453	13946
1970-JUL	1095	551	13990	1973-NOV	916	418	12701
1970-AUG	1204	646	14926	1973-DEC	992	419	10431
1970-SEP	1029	456	12900	1974-JAN	731	262	11616
1970-OCT	1147	475	12034	1974-FEB	665	299	10808
1970-NOV	1171	456	10643	1974-MAR	724	303	12421
1970-DEC	1299	468	10742	1974-APR	744	401	13605
1971-JAN	944	356	10266	1974-MAY	910	413	14455
1971-FEB	874	271	10281	1974-JUN	883	426	15019
1971-MAR	840	354	11527	1974-JUL	900	516	15662
1971-APR	893	427	12281	1974-AUG	1057	600	16745
1971-MAY	1007	465	13587	1974-SEP	1076	459	14717
1971-JUN	973	440	13049	1974-OCT	919	443	13756
1971-JUL	1097	539	16055	1974-NOV	920	412	12531
1971-AUG	1194	646	15220	1974-DEC	953	400	12568
1971-SEP	988	457	13824	1975-JAN	664	278	11249
1971-OCT	1077	446	12729	1975-FEB	607	302	11096
1971-NOV	1045	402	11467	1975-MAR	777	381	12637
1971-DEC	1115	441	11351	1975-APR	633	279	13018
1972-JAN	1005	359	10803	1975-MAY	791	442	15005
1972-FEB	857	334	10548	1975-JUN	790	409	15235
1972-MAR	879	312	12368	1975-JUL	803	416	15552
1972-APR	887	427	13311	1975-AUG	884	511	16905

date	front seat	rear seat	travel kms	date	front seat	rear seat	travel kms
1975-SEP	769	393	14776	1980-MAY	765	424	18117
1975-OCT	732	345	14104	1980-JUN	820	403	17552
1975-NOV	859	391	12854	1980-JUL	807	406	18299
1975-DEC	994	470	12956	1980-AUG	885	466	19361
1976-JAN	704	266	12177	1980-SEP	803	381	17924
1976-FEB	684	312	11918	1980-OCT	860	369	17872
1976-MAR	671	300	13517	1980-NOV	825	378	16058
1976-APR	643	373	14417	1980-DEC	911	392	15746
1976-MAY	771	412	15911	1981-JAN	704	284	15226
1976-JUN	644	322	15589	1981-FEB	691	316	14932
1976-JUL	828	458	16543	1981-MAR	688	321	16846
1976-AUG	748	427	17925	1981-APR	714	358	16854
1976-SEP	767	346	15406	1981-MAY	814	378	18146
1976-OCT	825	421	14601	1981-JUN	736	382	17559
1976-NOV	810	344	13107	1981-JUL	876	433	18655
1976-DEC	986	370	12268	1981-AUG	829	506	19453
1977-JAN	714	291	11972	1981-SEP	818	428	17923
1977-FEB	567	224	12028	1981-OCT	942	479	17915
1977-MAR	616	266	14033	1981-NOV	782	370	16496
1977-APR	678	338	14244	1981-DEC	823	349	13544
1977-MAY	742	298	15287	1982-JAN	595	238	13601
1977-JUN	840	386	16954	1982-FEB	673	285	15667
1977-JUL	888	479	17361	1982-MAR	660	324	17358
1977-AUG	852	473	17694	1982-APR	676	346	18112
1977-SEP	774	332	16222	1982-MAY	755	410	18581
1977-OCT	831	391	14969	1982-JUN	815	411	18759
1977-NOV	889	370	13624	1982-JUL	867	496	20668
1977-DEC	1046	431	13842	1982-AUG	933	534	21040
1978-JAN	889	366	12387	1982-SEP	798	396	18993
1978-FEB	626	250	11608	1982-OCT	950	470	18668
1978-MAR	808	355	15021	1982-NOV	825	385	16768
1978-APR	746	304	14834	1982-DEC	911	411	16551
1978-MAY	754	379	16565	1983-JAN	619	281	16231
1978-JUN	865	440	16882	1983-FEB	426	300	15511
1978-JUL	980	500	18012	1983-MAR	475	318	18308
1978-AUG	959	511	18855	1983-APR	556	391	17793
1978-SEP	856	384	17243	1983-MAY	559	398	19205
1978-OCT	798	366	16045	1983-JUN	483	337	19162
1978-NOV	942	432	14745	1983-JUL	587	477	20997
1978-DEC	1010	390	13726	1983-AUG	615	422	20705
1979-JAN	796	306	11196	1983-SEP	618	495	18759
1979-FEB	643	232	12105	1983-OCT	662	471	19240
1979-MAR	794	342	14723	1983-NOV	519	368	17504
1979-APR	750	329	15582	1983-DEC	585	345	16591
1979-MAY	809	394	16863	1984-JAN	483	296	16224
1979-JUN	716	355	16758	1984-FEB	434	319	16670
1979-JUL	851	385	17434	1984-MAR	513	349	18539
1979-AUG	931	463	18359	1984-APR	548	375	19759
1979-SEP	834	453	17189	1984-MAY	586	441	19584
1979-OCT	762	373	16909	1984-JUN	522	465	19976
1979-NOV	880	401	15380	1984-JUL	601	472	21486
1979-DEC	1077	466	15161	1984-AUG	644	521	21626
1980-JAN	748	306	14027	1984-SEP	643	429	20195
1980-FEB	593	263	14478	1984-OCT	641	408	19928
1980-MAR	720	323	16155	1984-NOV	711	490	18564
1980-APR	646	310	16585	1984-DEC	721	491	18149

APPENDIX D

UK price changes

date	price change	date	price change
1950-1	0.0084490544865279	1959-4	0.0105821093305369
1950-2	−0.0050487986543660	1960-1	0.0016181233304105
1950-3	0.0038461526886055	1960-2	−0.0022161098990638
1950-4	0.0214293914558992	1960-3	0.0054445227111829
1951-1	0.0232839389540449	1960-4	0.0128104233856403
1951-2	0.0299121323429455	1961-1	0.0079239717308917
1951-3	0.0379293285389640	1961-2	0.0031766212577034
1951-4	0.0212773984472849	1961-3	0.0171365771930149
1952-1	0.0270006018185058	1961-4	0.0138251049918425
1952-2	0.0140346711715057	1962-1	0.0121305505685076
1952-3	0.0112575217306222	1962-2	0.0109338371002675
1952-4	0.0109290705321903	1962-3	0.0010513250907626
1953-1	0.0088539683172550	1962-4	0.0014880955127019
1953-2	0.0034966658522944	1963-1	0.0169558061465560
1953-3	0.0023627259115981	1963-2	−0.0033302898966649
1953-4	0.0009732360865522	1963-3	−0.0017998056343648
1954-1	0.0038835000263977	1963-4	0.0095064701308285
1954-2	−0.0004528823156743	1964-1	0.0101376682844552
1954-3	0.0196473295718213	1964-2	0.0094758423054643
1954-4	0.0094608085042291	1964-3	0.0140211447248867
1955-1	0.0112360732669257	1964-4	0.0098040000966209
1955-2	0.0011711843376171	1965-1	0.0110881246904664
1955-3	0.0181931828441741	1965-2	0.0162381708431379
1955-4	0.0261393882030352	1965-3	0.0096136089566831
1956-1	0.0079752305743703	1965-4	0.0080267989494529
1956-2	0.0103805802278299	1966-1	0.0092838863100080
1956-3	0.0010280560188484	1966-2	0.0101169774642052
1956-4	0.0121423868257255	1966-3	0.0088440351770464
1957-1	0.0136988443581618	1966-4	0.0096681384730552
1957-2	−0.0037022279212015	1967-1	0.0063938836752557
1957-3	0.0180545215605451	1967-2	0.0001032615226096
1957-4	0.0158007445313437	1967-3	0.0005338840867116
1958-1	0.0049382816405825	1967-4	0.0132871299954331
1958-2	0.0051786958236232	1968-1	0.0155912107432541
1958-3	−0.0076447883188165	1968-2	0.0145713278135854
1958-4	0.0163268932874288	1968-3	0.0110867688006139
1959-1	0.0072610242370472	1968-4	0.0131817367020646
1959-2	−0.0191951645920371	1969-1	0.0212022076506031
1959-3	0.0013520310244529	1969-2	0.0070642343063755

UK price changes

date	price change	date	price change
1969-3	0.0085475311657376	1982-4	0.0076572844519269
1969-4	0.0142411976775678	1983-1	0.0049519999739722
1970-1	0.0190481949706944	1983-2	0.0127254485193250
1970-2	0.0151617430647947	1983-3	0.0196367663747411
1970-3	0.0170550754091731	1983-4	0.0114817150006719
1970-4	0.0228429587090599	1984-1	0.0058637707537912
1971-1	0.0274557520447654	1984-2	0.0128263136879202
1971-2	0.0264244321843404	1984-3	0.0157648196413390
1971-3	0.0195147486584831	1984-4	0.0124005131984548
1971-4	0.0145351396191131	1985-1	0.0125746558779243
1972-1	0.0166948785721703	1985-2	0.0268797663676002
1972-2	0.0092396314485979	1985-3	0.0091890175453887
1972-3	0.0224203685142349	1985-4	0.0049140148024289
1972-4	0.0257874502057387	1986-1	0.0068600206661635
1973-1	0.0185846056856334	1986-2	0.0066148920918364
1973-2	0.0222739735666356	1986-3	0.0072720769491554
1973-3	0.0214722812477185	1986-4	0.0126885933190888
1973-4	0.0358579525232807	1987-1	0.0116327023754623
1974-1	0.0416313834758135	1987-2	0.0095762452607891
1974-2	0.0485323461922063	1987-3	0.0082107849419403
1974-3	0.0309426125903717	1987-4	0.0107161278768428
1974-4	0.0459165989737005	1988-1	0.0048332621880194
1975-1	0.0595156501226990	1988-2	0.0175719935723567
1975-2	0.0811647817310722	1988-3	0.0202754753545044
1975-3	0.0493763472194563	1988-4	0.0202212772472334
1975-4	0.0356186790234685	1989-1	0.0162458446655789
1976-1	0.0367678608789195	1989-2	0.0219954787795547
1976-2	0.0266673169265613	1989-3	0.0157780062516547
1976-3	0.0294365225999917	1989-4	0.0196335798779765
1976-4	0.0460103056488332	1990-1	0.0175957618903793
1977-1	0.0505673588211266	1990-2	0.0392123740767577
1977-2	0.0343095760155300	1990-3	0.0227793019512109
1977-3	0.0226226190699194	1990-4	0.0154921766157710
1977-4	0.0154778877023167	1991-1	0.0053660535046385
1978-1	0.0183453133256850	1991-2	0.0149308220794474
1978-2	0.0178327965494397	1991-3	0.0107309634350358
1978-3	0.0244341357802717	1991-4	0.0096404157821741
1978-4	0.0172756554004234	1992-1	0.0051527533956559
1979-1	0.0321743570278561	1992-2	0.0148187052139855
1979-2	0.0267465059845203	1992-3	0.0055308342012944
1979-3	0.0720527654075770	1992-4	0.0043072571975804
1979-4	0.0286118473932619	1993-1	−0.0064678630074857
1980-1	0.0473115932904111	1993-2	0.0094870915838486
1980-2	0.0476589558588506	1993-3	0.0090848707858470
1980-3	0.0283462500655419	1993-4	0.0035323244075451
1980-4	0.0190315906164793	1994-1	0.0014094435032339
1981-1	0.0244504006677975	1994-2	0.0112024499512261
1981-2	0.0387816301941518	1994-3	0.0069418021721774
1981-3	0.0248700352276362	1994-4	0.0062047768868832
1981-4	0.0243422367363619	1995-1	0.0088950295688681
1982-1	0.0173385271622735	1995-2	0.0119752766503259
1982-2	0.0232646260176713	1995-3	0.0089220122778103
1982-3	0.0120010100385709	1995-4	0.0013333335308641

date	price change	date	price change
1996-1	0.0053156271343875	1999-1	−0.0042669982449910
1996-2	0.0062625109586168	1999-2	0.0046857104400285
1996-3	0.0082114259312180	1999-3	0.0068540471340416
1996-4	0.0058612997499914	1999-4	0.0072202479734873
1997-1	0.0058271450091931	2000-1	0.0041878613404744
1997-2	0.0065789123161647	2000-2	0.0120882837924579
1997-3	0.0157648196413382	2000-3	0.0080069550639669
1997-4	0.0081735758406412	2000-4	0.0064158866919071
1998-1	0.0031259794132925	2001-1	−0.0011634672632974
1998-2	0.0123034078957472	2001-2	0.0058994118100820
1998-3	0.0093090418470826	2001-3	0.0068248778542918
1998-4	0.0042669982449910	2001-4	−0.0011500863832374

Bibliography

Akaike, H. and G. Kitagawa (1999). *The Practice of Time Series Analysis*. New York: Springer-Verlag.

Anderson, B. D. O. and J. B. Moore (1979). *Optimal Filtering*. Englewood Cliffs: Prentice-Hall.

Bell, W. (2004). On RegComponents time series models and their applications. In A. C. Harvey, S. J. Koopman, and N. Shephard (Eds.), *State Space and Unobserved Components Models*. Cambridge: Cambridge University Press.

Belle, G. v. (2002). *Statistical Rules of Thumb*. New York: John Wiley & Sons, Inc.

Box, G. E. P. and G. M. Jenkins (1976). *Time Series Analysis*. San Francisco: Holden-Day.

Brockwell, P. J. and R. A. Davis (1987). *Time Series: Theory and Methods*. New York: Springer-Verlag.

____ ____ (2002). *Introduction to Time Series and Forecasting* (2nd edn.). New York: Springer-Verlag.

Chatfield, C. (2004). *The Analysis of Time Series. An Introduction* (6th edn.). London: Chapman & Hall/CRC.

Doornik, J. A. (2001). *Object-Oriented Matrix Programming using Ox 3.0*. London: Timberlake Consultants Press.

____ and M. Ooms (2002). *Introduction to Ox: An Object-Oriented Matrix Programming Language*. London: Timberlake Consultants Press.

Doucet, A., J. F. G. deFreitas, and N. J. Gordon (Eds.) (2000). *Sequential Monte Carlo Methods in Practice*. New York: Springer-Verlag.

Durbin, J. and S. J. Koopman (2001). *Time Series Analysis by State Space Methods*. Number 24 in Oxford Statistical Science Series. Oxford: Oxford University Press.

Hamilton, J. (1994). *Time Series Analysis*. Princeton: Princeton University Press.

Harvey, A. C. (1989). *Forecasting, Structural Time Series Models and the Kalman Filter*. Cambridge: Cambridge University Press.

____ (1993). *Time Series Models* (2nd edn.). Hemel Hempstead: Harvester Wheatsheaf.

____ and J. Durbin (1986). The effects of seat belt legislation on British road casualties: A case study in structural time series modelling. *Journal of the Royal Statistical Society A 149*(3), 187–227.

_____ and S. J. Koopman (1992). Diagnostic checking of unobserved components time series models. *J. Business and Economic Statist. 10*, 377–389.

_____ _____ and J. Penzer (1998). Messy time series. In T. B. Fomby and R. C. Hill (Eds.), *Advances in Econometrics, volume 13*, pp. 103–143. New York: JAI Press.

Kalman, R. E. (1960). A new approach to linear filtering and prediction problems. *J. Basic Engineering, Transactions ASMA Series D, 82*, 35–45.

Kirk, R. E. (1968). *Experimental Design: Procedures for the Behavioral Sciences.* Belmont, CA: Brooks/Cole.

Koopman, S. J., A. C. Harvey, J. A. Doornik, and N. Shephard (2000). *Stamp 6.0: Structural Time Series Analyser, Modeller and Predictor.* London: Timberlake Consultants.

_____ N. Shephard, and J. A. Doornik (1999). Statistical algorithms for models in state space using SsfPack 2.2. *Econometrics Journal 2*, 113–166.

Ord, K. and P. Young (2004). Estimating the impact of recent interventions on transportation indicators. *Journal of Transportation and Statistics 7*(1).

Ostrom, C. W. (1990). *Time Series Regression Techniques* (2nd edn.). London: Sage Publications.

Shumway, R. H. and D. S. Stoffer (2000). *Time Series Analysis and Its Applications.* New York: Springer-Verlag.

Stock, J. H. and M. Watson (1996). Evidence on structural instability in macroeconomic time series relations. *Journal of Business and Economic Statistics 14*, 11–30.

Varian, H. R. (1999). *Intermediate Microeconomics. A Modern Approach* (5th edn.). New York: W. W. Norton & Company.

West, M. and J. Harrison (1997). *Bayesian Forecasting and Dynamic Models* (2nd edn.). New York: Springer-Verlag.

Zivot, E. and J. Wang (2003). *Modelling Financial Time Series with S-PLUS.* New York: Springer-Verlag.

Index